POETRY TOWERS

20 23

CLASSROOM CREATIONS

EDITED BY DAISY JOB

First published in Great Britain in 2023 by:

Young Writers
Remus House
Coltsfoot Drive
Peterborough
PE2 9BF
Telephone: 01733 890066
Website: www.youngwriters.co.uk

Printed and bound in the UK by BookPrintingUK
Website: www.bookprintinguk.com
YB0555H

FOREWORD

For Young Writers' latest competition we invited primary school pupils to enroll at a new school, Poetry Towers, where they could let their imaginations roam free.

At Poetry Towers the timetable of subjects on offer is unlimited, so pupils could choose any topic that inspired them and write in any poetry style. We provided free resources including lesson plans, poetry guides and inspiration and examples to help pupils craft a piece of writing they can be proud of.

Here at Young Writers our aim is to encourage creativity in children and to inspire a love of the written word, so it's great to get such an amazing response, with some absolutely fantastic poems. It's important for children to express themselves and a great way to engage them is to allow them to write about what they care about. The result is a varied collection of poems with a range of styles and techniques that showcase their creativity and writing ability.

We'd like to congratulate all the young poets in this anthology, the latest alumni of the Young Writers' academy of poetry and rhyme. We hope this inspires them to continue with their creative writing.

CONTENTS

Kwadwo Yeboah Amoabeng (9)	61
Migina Ghale (8)	62
Sophia Sousa	63
Wojtek Chabera (9)	64
Archie Christopher Spraggs	65
Amber Knight (9)	66
Ayda Lily Dugtig (9)	67
Morgan Aird (8)	68

Halfway Primary School, Llanelli

Jessica Wilson (10)	69
Cai Thomas (10)	70
Albie Beard (9)	71
Isla Jenkins (10)	72
Noah Evans (10)	73
Freya Thomas (9)	74
Dexter Jones (10)	75
George Jones-John (10)	76
Poppy Beynon (10)	77
Ethan Baker (9)	78

Longridge Towers School, Berwick-Upon-Tweed

Ezra Kerr (10)	79
Amelia Davidson (10)	80
Oliver Brunton (10)	83
Eden Watson (10)	84
Clemmie Graham-Campbell (10)	86
Esme Mitchell (9)	88
Jake Stephens (10)	90
Tom Parmenter (10)	92
Erin Macfarlane (10)	93
Lukas Rowlands (10)	94
Giles Gibb (9)	95
Harry Cairns (10)	96
Oliver van Boeckel van Rumpt (10)	97
Charlie Baird (10)	98
Paulien Wagner (9)	99
Ihsan Saygilier (10)	100
Maisie Wilson (10)	101
Rocco Lindsay (10)	102

Poppy Douglas (10)	103
Harvey Mcdonald (10)	104
Wren Pearson (10)	105
Ruby Richardson (10)	106

Milldene Primary School, Tiptree

Martha Francis (8)	107
Benjamin Lucas (8)	108
Lily Bonnyhood (8)	110
Kieran Grimwade (8)	111
Phoebe Herman (7)	112
Rosie Terry (8)	113
Hallie Coney (8)	114
Yaqub Al-Mahfuz (8)	115
Max Fletcher (8)	116

St Bernard's RC Primary School, Ellesmere Port

Lydia Minshull (8)	117
Sadie Whitfield (9)	118
Brooke Fairweather-Barry (8)	119
Sofia Perkins (9)	120
Emilia Mae Fitzgerald (9)	121
Texas Sweeney (9)	122
Esmai Cooper (9)	123

St Mary's CE Primary School, Sheffield

Ellie Garrod (9)	124
Faith Masaba-Kituyi (9)	125
Tia Shanice Stacey Thompson (8)	126
Connie Ovenden (8)	127
Sally Bola (9)	128
Venuhya Reddy Neelam (9)	129
Lillie-Lovélle Melville (9)	130
Abdwadood Qasim (9)	131
Dominic Gregory (9)	132
Juliette Hart (9)	133
Grace Woods (8)	134
Tom Mason (9)	135

THE POEMS

Spring

A haiku

Spring trees blossoming
Flowers blooming in the sun
Ice cream dribbling.

Aaron Mc (8)

Friends

Friends are like flowers, they brighten your day.
Friends are like lights, they light up your world.
Friends can make you happy because they always do their best to cheer you up.
Friends can make you happy because at play time they offer to play with you when you're lonely.
Friends can make you feel better when you've just sprained your ankle.
Friends will always be there when you're sad.
You can have as many friends as you like.
Friends will always be there to support you.
You can do anything when you have a friend with you.
You can laugh with them, sing with them
And you can play with them...
Friends are the best.
Friendship never ends.

Mae Negus (7)
Comberbach Primary School, Comberbach

Elemental

Shiver

Frozen basilisks left and right
Chewed to bits by a double snap
His shell prevents their killing glare

Seed

His horns tangled with a basilisk's teeth
Leaves gouged into the snake's eyes
The growth roars, vine leeches in

Shock

Jolting the serpent off
Slicing off its tail
Pulsing a blast from his mouth

Scorch

Erupting and burning
Heavy fire breath
Arrogant tail swipe.

Dominic Raeburn (8)
Comberbach Primary School, Comberbach

A Boy Called Harry

Harry Potter was capable of amazing magic,
The scar on his head was a reminder of something tragic.
Hogwarts Castle was where Harry felt most at home,
Although when Harry saw Malfoy it made him groan.
His best friends, Ron and Hermione, were always there,
To help him in trouble, to laugh and to care.
He and his friends fight against Voldemort,
Using all the special magic that they were taught.

William Malam (8)
Comberbach Primary School, Comberbach

True Friends

Best friends stick together till the end
They are like a straight line that does not bend
They trust each other forever
No matter if you are apart you are together
They can be your hero and save the day
They will never leave your side, they are here to
stay
They will help you up when you fall
Your true friends are best of all.

Cody Hartley-Chambers (8)
Comberbach Primary School, Comberbach

A War Rages In Space

Suddenly, a galactic cruiser came into view,
Time to jump into lightspeed,
All rebel fighters head to Hoth,
Ready to take and destroy the AT-ATs.

Whilst preparing to defend the base,
An Empire scout spots Echo Base,
Rebels went straight for it,
Shooting down the spider-like robot; a close call.

Zachary Doerr (8)
Comberbach Primary School, Comberbach

Riddle

They are rarely white,
Many are fluffy and grey,
There are some red ones,
The rarest are the white ones,
They live in forests and woodlands,
They eat nuts, acorns and lots more,
There are about 14,000 red ones,
There are some native red ones.
What are they?

Answer: Squirrels.

Sophie Woodcock (8)
Comberbach Primary School, Comberbach

Football

Football is great,
I play it with my mates.
We run, we tackle, we score
But we always want more.
Watching Darwin with his pace,
He will always win the race.
Mo Salah runs down the wing,
As the crowds continue to sing...
Mo Salah, Mo Salah, the Egyptian king.

Lucas Burke (7)
Comberbach Primary School, Comberbach

Guinea Pig, Guinea Pig

Guinea pig, guinea pig,
Fluffy and cute,
Guinea pig, guinea pig,
Squeaky like a flute,
Guinea pig, guinea pig,
Eats all the fruit,
Guinea pig, guinea pig,
The fruit comes from roots.

Lily Marshall (8)
Comberbach Primary School, Comberbach

When I Grow Up

When I grow up...
I want to have a dog,
I want to be famous,
I'll be a star,
I'll be so fit and strong,
I'll be a famous gymnast.

Niamh Tomlinson (8)

Comberbach Primary School, Comberbach

Earth

I am enormous
Floating through space
A giant ball of rock
I am mainly water (71%)
An amazing ball of life
Turning slowly
What am I?

Stanley Jones (8)
Comberbach Primary School, Comberbach

Tortoise

My armour is as hard as rock
My skin is as fragile as paper
I feed on the sun's energy.
What am I?

Bear Cook (8)
Comberbach Primary School, Comberbach

Rose

A haiku

Red, riveting rose
Lying in the sunlight so
Precious red ruby.

Matthew Ollier (7)

Comberbach Primary School, Comberbach

Niagara Falls

A haiku

The Niagara Falls
A beautiful place to be
A nice place to see.

Bella Hiorns Vipond (7)

Comberbach Primary School, Comberbach

Spain

We like to go to Spain to get away from the rain.
We splash around in the pool, have fun, enjoying
ourselves in the sun.
We love to go to the beach and play in the sea
One time I even spotted my friend Leigh.
At quiet times we sit in the garden
And me and Wyatt play mermaids.
At lunch we sit in the shade and I love all the
games that we play.
We go to town on a train all the way there and
back again.
My favourite dinner is Chinese
My normal order is rice, chicken and peas.
Sometimes I swim at night until they turn off all
the lights.
Some evenings we sit on the beach and eat fish
and chips
And we look out at all the fishing ships.
I can't wait to go back again to the holidays
That we have had in Spain.

Ellisa Newberry (9)

Coteford Junior School, Eastcote

When I Grow Up

When I grow up I can't wait to see,
All the amazing things that I could be.
An artist or a singer, an acrobat or a teacher,
The possibilities are endless, I'll always be a
dreamer.
I want to fly high up in the sky,
Reach up to the stars or maybe travel to Mars.
Back down on Earth adventures await me,
Exploring towns and cities and sunbathing under
tropical trees.
But most of all I hope to be surrounded by my
loved ones,
Showered with hugs and kisses.
Life can be anything you hope it to be
So keep on believing and you may just get what
you wished for.

Juhi Chudasama (8)
Coteford Junior School, Eastcote

Dragons And Sharks

In a magical world, let's have some fun,
With dragons and sharks under the sun!

Dragons fly very high,
With giant wings in the sky.

Sharks swim deep in the sea,
With sharp teeth, they're as cool as can be!

Dragons are brave, strong and not very true,
But they are kind, they'll protect me and you!

Dragons and sharks, let's use our imagination,
We'll have so much fun in our celebration!

Ali Moshen (9)
Coteford Junior School, Eastcote

Summer

The sun rises early,
And you're going to a beach,

Swimming all day,
Munching all the ice lollies away,

Having a bright lovely evening,
Singing a nice song,

You go to bed and the next day
It's going to be a big and magnificent day!

The next day,
It's extremely burning
Put on a lot of suncream,
Sit in the shade,

Run around the
Beautiful blossoms,
Go and have
A cool drink,

Take a walk off to
The park,
Laugh and enjoy
With family and friends.

Mahroush Rahimi (9)
Coteford Junior School, Eastcote

The Shimmering Ocean

The sunshine shimmers
In the ocean like a mirror
Dolphins jump up high through the sky
And flying fish fly
In the ocean like flies
Beautiful shimmers shimmer
In the ocean like a mirror
Clownfish are dancing like clowns
And dance on their own
And the kids dance with their clone
And jellyfish happily dance
Like a big jelly with their jelly wellies
People's love spreads all around
Like all people spin around.

Lojain Saeed (9)
Coteford Junior School, Eastcote

Starlight

S himmering, shining stars twinkling in the midnight sky

T umbling down as fast as a bullet

A nd when the sun comes up to play

R elaxation for the day

L onging to come out and shine at night

I t's finally time to delight, be bright, what a sight

G littering like a silver sparkler

H igh, high, high up

T ime to shine again, forever, in the magical sky.

Mason Sejpal (9)
Coteford Junior School, Eastcote

A Dull, Grey, Rainy Day

It's a dull, grey, rainy day.
I just can't think of what to play.
Maybe a game?
Mmmm, no.
Maybe a book?
Mmmm, no.
Maybe cook?
Mmmm, no.
It's a dull, grey, rainy day.
And I still can't think of what to play.
I wish I could go outside.
Maybe to the seaside.
It's a dull, grey, rainy day.
Please help me think of what to play.

Josh Lieberman (9)
Coteford Junior School, Eastcote

All About Family

F amily are the people who take care of you, like your parents or siblings.

A family can have a stepdad, mum, sister or brother.

M any people can be adopted. Adopted means you're in a family but not your real one.

I love my family, just like you love yours.

L ove people that are your family

Y ou guys, thank you for listening.

Samuel (9)
Coteford Junior School, Eastcote

Fly Like A Butterfly

Fly like a butterfly,
Roar like a lion.
Fly elegantly,
Roar fiercely.

You are great,
You are strong.
But there's one thing you're missing,
You're missing one of your kind.

Search the trees,
Search the stars.
Will you find them?
Nobody knows.

Fly like a butterfly,
Roar like a lion.

Rayaan Ahmed (8)
Coteford Junior School, Eastcote

Christmas

C old winter nights
H ear snow crunching
R obins roam the sky
I cicles all around
S oft, sparkly snow coating the field
T insel wrapped around the tree
M arshmallows floating in hot chocolate
A nd the clock ticking till midnight
S anta is here with his reindeer!

Robyn Bray (9)
Coteford Junior School, Eastcote

Devon

D ays in Devon are fun and divine, eating ice creams and having a good time

E xploring the caves, trying to be brave

V enture off into the field, adventures as we climb the hills

O n a sunny day, the beach is never far away

N ever ever want to leave because I miss that Devon air I breathe.

Kyle Warner (9)
Coteford Junior School, Eastcote

Animals And Me

Down behind a dustbin
I met a dog called Flo
Who was so fluffy
She had to wear a bow.

Jelly, jelly, jelly,
My cat's called Melly
And she loves
A scratch on the belly.

Snakes, snakes, snakes,
Are stupid enough to sneeze
In front of Suzie (they love her).

Florence Francis (9)
Coteford Junior School, Eastcote

Dr Who

D r Who
O rdinary people go on an adventure
C an we go time travelling?
T ime travelling is fun!
O dd creatures all around
R un quickly!

W ho is The Doctor?
H ow do we stop the Daleks from invading?
O bey the Cybermen!

Tallulah McNab (9)
Coteford Junior School, Eastcote

The Beautiful Game

On the grassy field they run
Their training, it's never done
The ball in play, the game has begun
Crowds shouting, "Go score a ton."

Kicking, dribbling, passing fine
To the goal they draw the line
The keeper on watch all the time
Saving shots with grace divine.

Ahmed Osman
Coteford Junior School, Eastcote

Flowers And Daisies

Flowers
I love flowers because they are colourful
When petals fall
I feel so calm
You're never alone
Flowers are alive
Daisies
I love daisies because they are pretty
When petals fall
You have good fortune
You're never alone
Daisies are alive.

Zhor Naceur (8)
Coteford Junior School, Eastcote

The Falcon

The falcon spreads his wings...
Surprise!
A feather falls from the sky.
Gushing past the sky so high.
I gaze back and see the blue-grey sky
And suddenly, I escape the park.
Gliding through the wind at dark.
My mind is full of wonder at this marvellous bird.

Dilan Naran (9)
Coteford Junior School, Eastcote

The Robin On The Wind

A robin soaring through the sky,
Flying like a feather in the wind,
Hunting for food in silver-white snow.
Their red chests shiny in the sky
Their wings beating in the pure sun.

Robin, be free,
Robin, follow the wind,
Robin, fly high.

Jack Alford (9)
Coteford Junior School, Eastcote

Monsters On Halloween Night

It's a Halloween night
And the monsters are waiting to give you a fright
Trick or treat, we just want the treats
The ghosts will steal your toast
So remember to check under your bed
Because the monsters will come
And now the poem is done.

Neelam Wessal (9)
Coteford Junior School, Eastcote

Fly Little Robin

Fly little robin, in the trees
Fly little tit, who loves bird feed
Dance little fox, in the autumn leaves
Swim little fish, in the diamond streams
Sleep little hedgehog, for tomorrow's new
Play little children, this world is for you.

Vivienne Vozila (9)
Coteford Junior School, Eastcote

Flags

I like flags
I like to know them
So today I wrote a poem.
All the countries have a flag
Which flies up for people's land.
Different colours,
Different meanings.
All of them are made of feelings.

Andrei Barboi
Coteford Junior School, Eastcote

Arsenal

Although I like the carnival,
I'd rather be watching Arsenal.
While I'm eating KFC,
I'll be watching Arsenal FC.
Even though Mr Harding likes Spurs,
Arsenal come back and occur!

Leo Stevens-Wallace (9)
Coteford Junior School, Eastcote

Football

A football is round
And it shows who I am
So get together
And play to your heart's desires.

Football is a game
And you get fame
Only by playing truly happily!

Jack Maxwell
Coteford Junior School, Eastcote

Family

My family, they are really kind and loyal
And they always are on my side
Even though we fight
I will always
And they will always
Be on mine and their side.

Samantha Belinga (9)
Coteford Junior School, Eastcote

I Am A Footballer

I can take a pass in a crowded playground
Run or pass, you don't want to finish last
The kick always starts the game to be won
The real fun is when I have won.

Jack Peacock (9)
Coteford Junior School, Eastcote

My Best Friend

I have a friend and his name is Kyle
He's not just my normal friend
He's my best friend
Whenever I get hurt
He's always by my side.

Aron (9)
Coteford Junior School, Eastcote

Rugby In My Blood

S coring a try
T rying my best
A lways puts me to the test
R ugby is the very best.

Romeo-Beau Burkett (9)

Coteford Junior School, Eastcote

Bluebell

B ulb, bright indigo, iconic and enchanting.

L ight of the night, a favourite among the fairies.

U nder and over, soft like velvet are the bell bottles.

E very year in springtime, woodland floors transform.

B rilliant, bright indigo petals, the white and purple beauty.

E nter the woods with care, for you may be enveloped, drowned by the hue.

L ightly tread, or the bells will ring, coming down, bringing darkness.

L ike the bluebells, the lady's nightcap, the wood bells are singing beautifully.

Louis William Allen (9)
Dunmore Primary School, Abingdon

Dandelion

D on't pick me it won't be easy.

A nd spin me around in a time machine.

N othing stops my twisty, tangly roots that you will never escape from.

D own at the bottom of the garden a dandelion is a mini sun for you.

E very dandelion has its own shine.

L ion's tooth leaves pointed and jagged.

I have a favourite plant now and it's a dandelion.

O verall a dandelion is one of the most delicate plants in our world.

N ow it's coming to an end now to leave.

Kaiden Dodd (9)

Dunmore Primary School, Abingdon

Bluebell

B lue as a carpet, tick-tock, the clock is ticking

L ight is shining, tick-tock in the light

U nderneath the wet, soggy dirt, tick-tock the roots are growing

E nchanting light glows blue on the bluebells. Tick-tock, the bees are coming

B ees are here to blossom. Tick-tock to the buzzing

E vil magic, tick-tock fairies are hiding

L uring you in to pick a flower

L ost forever in the bluebells. Tick-tock, the bluebells are gone.

Chloe Begley (9)
Dunmore Primary School, Abingdon

Dandelion

D azzle me with your light,

A ll around the lawn your head shines happily in the sun,

N ot that you are a weed, but gardeners pick at you,

D ancing in the wind, blowing my seeds, scattering all around.

E verywhere my parachutes land, spreading my joy.

L ion's tooth I am called, but to you I am a pest.

I survive in lawns you mow, my head pokes out once again.

O pen at day, close at night.

N ever call me a weed, I am beautiful just as me.

Eva Hurst (9)

Dunmore Primary School, Abingdon

Dandelion

D andelion you are brilliant the way you open in the morning and close at night.

A nd you shine in the green grass.

N ever would I call you a weed.

D andelion, you help us survive.

E very ant has to wear sunglasses you dazzle them so much.

L et new names take root, thrive and grow!

I would change your name, such as the bane of law perfectionists.

O r fallen star of the football pitch or scatter seed.

N ever would I call you a weed.

Elliot Draper-Rodi (9)
Dunmore Primary School, Abingdon

Bluebell

B luebell, that's me, people call me blue battle, wood bells.

L iving on the floor of Bluebell Wood, be careful where you stand.

U nder the forest floor I grow.

E very day I shine, my head held high.

B ut people say I look like a fairy hat.

E nter my forest of blue, it's as deep as the ocean.

L and is swamped in a carpet of blue.

L ost in a hidden world for humans to explore.

Lacy James
Dunmore Primary School, Abingdon

Bluebell

B luebell, oh bluebell
L ong beautiful heads that dance in the springtime
U p your stem grows high in the sky
E veryone loves your carpet of blue
B luebell, oh you beautiful bluebell
E veryone comes to see your beauty as you shine in the April sun
L et me keep you
L ady's nightcap, your flower opens, lovely spring flower, let me see you again soon.

Jay Mcdowell (9)
Dunmore Primary School, Abingdon

Bluebell

B lue carpet across the woodland floor,
L ight shines bright on each flower,
U nder, in dark, damp places,
E very day you look outside to see the wonderful blue flower,
B right colours bring joy and happiness,
E very day there are more,
L ilac flowers lighten up the forest floor,
L ight and soft and beautiful, like a delicate fairy house.

Olivia Forder (9)

Dunmore Primary School, Abingdon

Dandelion

D azzle little flower,
A little clock to blow,
N o! I'll never call you a weed,
D andelion, you beautiful little flower,
E ver so bright, sunny and yellow,
L ittle time machine you are,
I 'll never ever pick you, I'll leave you to rest,
O h goodness, such a tasty, edible flower,
N ew dandelions grow every day.

Maksymilian Helliwell (9)
Dunmore Primary School, Abingdon

Bramble

B ramble is spiky, bramble is smooth.

R olling round the town.

A ll thorns grabbing the paths and walls as it climbs.

M oving like a snake in the grass, its giraffe-like head climbs over walls.

B ringing fruit and joy on autumn days.

L iving long and people loving its life.

E ating berries in a bowl full of black juice, but the best bit is hot steaming blackberry crumble.

Zoe Ackroyd
Dunmore Primary School, Abingdon

Dandelion

D andelion

A n army grows on, the seeds ride the wind,

N ever would I call it a weed,

D ancing on the breeze,

E ver so shining yellow,

L ong live the dandelion,

I 'll never remove you from my garden again,

O h, my garden, you'll grow once again,

N ew dandelions emerge from blades of grass,

S hining their yellow heads for all to see.

Gautham Matam (8)

Dunmore Primary School, Abingdon

Ivy Leaf

I am Ivy, an evergreen plant.

V enturing the walls, fences and trees with my dark green leaves.

Y ou think we aren't special? What about glowing veins? Also,

L uscious leaves may be emerald-green. We are,

E legant, smooth with a strangling stem and,

A s we curl around the trees, walls and buildings.

F ragile leaves ripping may be thin or pulling.

Dristi Thapa (9)

Dunmore Primary School, Abingdon

Ivy Grows

I 'll see you anywhere, from backyards to forests.
V ines, your beautiful vines, sticking to the tree.
Y ellow lines as bright as the sun.

G reat coverage like a blanket.
R eigns over the wild forest.
O ver cities to caves, spreading silently.
W hy do people not like you?
S haped like a heart, trying to gain our heart!

Caitlin McLeod (9)
Dunmore Primary School, Abingdon

Bramble

B ranching, twisting, arching, flying.

R eaching out to pierce you.

A rching and whipping, taking over.

M ucking up the forest floor.

B ramble, creatures it may be.

L onely caterpillars graze on furry leaves, as blackbirds peck on purple berries in the sun.

E nveloping the walls with spiky thorns.

James Burford (9)

Dunmore Primary School, Abingdon

Lost Love

Across the block it waits for you,
A place that makes you feel blue.

It's a place that makes you feel glum.
It's sad not happy, no pets, no family, nobody
around to help.
Gloomy, gloomy, gloomy.
The gloomy place has a fire.
No money to get someone to hire.

Gloomy, gloomy, gloomy, gloomy.
Going there will help you know how others feel
when they feel glum.

Henry Larkins (8)
Dunmore Primary School, Abingdon

Dandelions

D andelions, as bright as the sun,

A mazing golden head sprout as petals.

N o more known as Dent-De-Lion,

D azzling everywhere, anywhere.

E ven though they are beautiful,

L ife can be a bit cruel...

I f you see a dandelion,

O ver the hedge or over the hill,

N o! Don't call it a weed!

Mingsa Wanem (9)

Dunmore Primary School, Abingdon

Bluebell

B luebell forest in the April sun
L ying, a blanket of blue on the ground
U nbelievable flowers dazzle around
E ver silent on the floor
B lue like the sea
E ver found in the forest
L onely like a worm in the ground the bluebell sways in the wind
L ovely like fragile gems that brighten the day.

Frederick Obeng Jr
Dunmore Primary School, Abingdon

Ivy

I am Ivy, I crawl and climb.

V ia bark and stone, I strangle and cling.

Y ou think we are a pain, we are just doing our thing.

L ying on floors and walls, we hold on tight.

E vergreen we are.

A round walls our smooth leaves look like hearts.

F ragile and shiny we are here for a reason.

Katya Chapman (9)
Dunmore Primary School, Abingdon

Ivy

I vy is my friend, she's like a

V est of green covering the tree

Y ou and I both know she's a weed but look closer and see.

V enom is in her blood; she'll pounce when she wants.

I would never insult her!

N ot once, not ever

E vergreen is she and in my mind she's the queen.

Catherine Hall (9)

Dunmore Primary School, Abingdon

Bluebells

B lue carpets of flowers
L ost in the deep woods.
U nder giant trees that give shelter and protect.
E very flower dances in the strong wind.
B ells that ring quietly.
E ven small ants walk
L onely deer jump high through.
L oving the sea of blue.

Kwadwo Yeboah Amoabeng (9)
Dunmore Primary School, Abingdon

Ivy Leaf

I vy grows along your wall,
V ines come out at dawn,
Y ou can see me creeping over your lawn.

L eaves, glossy and green, have been seen,
E aten by butterflies, that's very mean.
A ll day gardeners,
F ight me, that's no problem I will win!

Migina Ghale (8)
Dunmore Primary School, Abingdon

Land Of Blue

Across the lake
A gloomy town
A place they call Blue.
A town of blue.
All of the people are gloomy
They're not happy
They are sad
They sit alone
Hungry and gloomy
The sea is cold
Shivering like ice
It is blue.
More than ever.

Sophia Sousa
Dunmore Primary School, Abingdon

Bramble

B ramble arching across the woods.
R eaching out to take over.
A cross the city floor popping car tyres.
M ocking the forest with thorns.
B ramble arching across the wood.
L ong thorns take over the world.
E nd of the world has come.

Wojtek Chabera (9)

Dunmore Primary School, Abingdon

Dandelion

D andelion
A beautiful flower
N eeds water and food
D andy yellow sunshine head
E ats soil and roots
L ovely stem
I don't know if it's dangerous
O h it's so nice
N o, it's just a flower.

Archie Christopher Spraggs
Dunmore Primary School, Abingdon

The Sands Of Blue

The powerless person with a sad face,
Makes it all gloomy.
The light is out of reach, dark, sketchy,
It never goes anywhere,
No matter what happens.
The mysterious man came from nowhere,
No one knows.
They will never know.

Amber Knight (9)
Dunmore Primary School, Abingdon

Sunset On The Water

Sunset on the water
Dark, gloomy, pitiful, alone, sadness on the horizon
Moans of grief, trees withering away, forgotten
Waters black and grimy boats creaking with sorrow
Screams echoing on the waters.

Ayda Lily Dugtig (9)
Dunmore Primary School, Abingdon

Ivy

I   twist and turn all around trees, walls and fences

V ery strong, my roots grip hard

Y ou find me hard to rip off as my heart-shaped
     leaves grow bigger and stronger.

Morgan Aird (8)

Dunmore Primary School, Abingdon

Stich And Angel

S mall steps at a time
T o take you to the world
I nto the forest
C an you feel the love?
H ave you heard the tweets of the birds?

A lways stay together
N ever ever nasty
D ozing under the stars

A lways happy
N ever lost
G azing at each other
E ager to be with each other
L ittle buddies.

Jessica Wilson (10)
Halfway Primary School, Llanelli

The Night Fox

It scutters through the forest, munching on some chicken.
It smells prey, a bell rings every time to catch its prey.
It hunts every night, its secret is unknown.
It howls like a wolf, this scares humans nearby, especially when it's night-time.
The clouds turn black, the time to hunt and feast.
It howls every night to smell different animals to catch.

Cai Thomas (10)
Halfway Primary School, Llanelli

Football

F ootball is a really good sport
O h, you don't have to play for a team
O h, you don't have to like football
T o join football you need to sign up to
B e able to play football
A nd be a professional
L earn new tricks like a rainbow flick
L earn some more tricks like a Ronaldo chop.

Albie Beard (9)
Halfway Primary School, Llanelli

Space, 4.6 Billion Years Ago!

There were no ups
There were no downs
There was no side to side
There was no light
There was no dark
There was no shape of any kind
There were no stars
Or Planet Mars
There were no ups
There were no downs
There was no time
So there were no passing hours, days or minutes in our lovely universe.

Isla Jenkins (10)
Halfway Primary School, Llanelli

Expectations And Dreams

E xcellent dreams

X -ray dreams

P lanning your dreams

E njoyable dreams

C alm dreams

T rust your dreams

A mazing dreams

T rustworthy dreams

I nspirational dreams

O ptimistic dreams

N atural dreams

S pecific dreams.

Noah Evans (10)

Halfway Primary School, Llanelli

A Recipe For A Good Friend

A recipe for a good friend is kindness and love.
In a good friendship trust is a must.
But sometimes trust is not a must.
Sadly sometimes people as little as mice are not always nice.
People who remind us always have kindness.
Everyone who's sunny make it always sunny!

Freya Thomas (9)
Halfway Primary School, Llanelli

Safety

S tay with a trusted adult
A lways feel safe
F eel free
E veryone should feel safe
T here are age restrictions for good reasons
Y ou should always feel safe wherever you are.

Dexter Jones (10)

Halfway Primary School, Llanelli

Nature's Beauty

The blue sky,
The green grass,
The flowers across the lands,
The rabbits hopping,
The birds tweeting,
The fish in the ponds,
The frogs hopping across the hills and mountains,
Nature's beauty.

George Jones-John (10)
Halfway Primary School, Llanelli

Cats

C uddly all the time
A mazing at jumping
T errifying sometimes
S oft and cute.

Poppy Beynon (10)
Halfway Primary School, Llanelli

Seagulls

A haiku

The seagulls flying
One seagull chilling in a
Tree, waiting for spring.

Ethan Baker (9)

Halfway Primary School, Llanelli

Lobster Poem

I saw a lobster and the lobster saw me,
So I said, "Hi" and he said hi back to me,
So I brought him to Yo Sushi,
I said, "You know what this is?" He said, "No."
I said it's his mother, he said, "It's my brother."

So I phoned animal cruelty,
Yes, I phoned the company,
I said, "You know what this is?"
They said no. I said, "It's his mother, oh wait,
It's his brother."

They said, "We can't change the food,
It would be rather rude."
"So give us that lobster and we'll be on our way,"
I said, "You killed his brother and want his mother."

Ezra Kerr (10)
Longridge Towers School, Berwick-Upon-Tweed

The Homosapiens

On a hot summer's day
We arrived at school
We couldn't find our teachers
Which was not cool!
We looked up high and we looked down low
In the office and even the old swimming pool
All of a sudden someone shouted out
"Look, what's that over there!"
Charging over the roundabout
Then I cried out, "Everybody, hide!"
We ran to the classroom so we could survive.

We looked through the window
And we could see
Hundreds of aliens
Roaming free
Some were red, some were blue
Some had crazy green hair too
With arms like spaghetti
And multiple eyes
We looked at each other

With a look of surprise
We put on our shin guards
And mouth guards blue
We grabbed our hockey sticks
And cricket bats too

We all worked together
And came up with a plan
We had to fight the aliens
And this is how it began
We knew that they loved
Mashed potato and peas
So we ran under cover
Hiding behind trees
To the kitchen we fled
To fill trays and buckets
Of their most favourite food
Including some nuggets
Armed with our buckets
We dolloped the mash
On the ground spaced out
Along the grassy path

We sped back to the classroom
To watch the rest unfold
The mash was too irresistible
For the aliens to behold
As quick as a flash
They devoured the mash
Which led them on a trail
To the rusty old bus, Mabel
Mabel's door slammed shut
The aliens were trapped
We had tricked those pesky creatures
"Hooray!" we cheered and clapped
We found the teachers
Quivering with fright
They were so happy to be rescued
Despite the school being a bombsight

Yippee, we had saved the day!
Thank goodness the lessons could resume without delay!
Then we looked to the sky
And saw Mabel flying away!

Amelia Davidson (10)

Longridge Towers School, Berwick-Upon-Tweed

Electronics

"No electronics! Don't watch TV!"
My parents keep shouting at me.
"Get fresh air, go outside,
Read a book, exercise!
It makes you bad, it rots your brain,
Your vocabulary will go down the drain!"

They may be right about it all
But when I watch I have a ball!
YouTube shorts and Roblox Bedwars
Mario Kart and Minecraft ores.
So many different things to see
Memes and pranks for eternity!

You go to school and work your brain
So much so it drives you insane!
When you get home you want to play
For all the hours of the day.
So no more homework or nagging me
There are electronics to play, so let me be!

Oliver Brunton (10)
Longridge Towers School, Berwick-Upon-Tweed

Exciting Dreams

Theo the toad is a pioneer
He jumps up high and gazes out at the sky
Trees and flowers watch him leap
He wants to find a new home
He hears Europa is nice
It has cool waters under the ice
So when engines blaze and fires burn
He jumps at the window
Of the rocket to learn
How to get there and how to live
So far away from Earth
And to have a home of his own, happily alone.

Luna is a bat who marvels at the moon
She knows that if she wants
She could learn about it soon
Every night she catches bugs and flies
To bring home to eat a marvellous feast
But she still longs for the moon
Some nights she sits and watches
As preparations for rocket launches

Take place where she lives
One night she goes and sleeps
On the fuel tank of the rocket's side
But on that night the engines roared
And the rocket soared up, up and away
And Luna's dreams to become a space bat came
alive.

On a blazing hot day
A steady sloth named Gerald made his way
To a launch pad with a rocket by the ESA
He came to be a cameraman
And would ask every camera that he passed
About what they saw
And the cameras replied that
They see blazing fires and flags for empires
But mostly the fiery sun
And the stunning star clusters
Of the night sky.

Eden Watson (10)
Longridge Towers School, Berwick-Upon-Tweed

The Whispering Tree

O that grand old whispering tree
I go there and it whispers to me
It tells me tales of stormy sails
And curses with following doom
A dragon without its peppermint breath
And a witch without her broom
It told me of trees that grew no leaves
And words I can't understand
And a one-eyed crone who lived alone
With a foot instead of a hand.

O that grand old whispering tree
I go there and it sings to me
It tells me of the things it's seen
Of creatures kind and creatures mean
It told me of a while ago
When the trees would start to grow
Of the animals that are extinct
The vandalor and the dunderthink
And of strange people who like to play
With shields and swords made out of clay.

O that grand old whispering tree
I go there and it speaks to me
It said that it had come before
The dodo and the dinosaur
It is the oldest plant alive
And the longest to survive
Waves of knowledge spread around
From its roots into the ground
And if you're hurt or in despair
The whispering tree is always there.

Clemmie Graham-Campbell (10)
Longridge Towers School, Berwick-Upon-Tweed

The Spring Garden

I pull my curtains back and see the sun as bright as
a gold coin glistening overhead.
The blue sky is like an ocean sparkling on a sandy
beach.
The sound of the singing birds is as joyful as a
happy conversation.
Pushing open the window the scent of fresh air hits
me like a wave crashing over me.

Excitedly I dress and run down the stairs as fast as
a raindrop racing down the window pane.
Outside I see never-ending fields of yellow, the
colour of stars, and a mix of lush greens.
It's as if an artist has splattered paint all over the
canvas of the countryside.

Barefoot, I feel the grass tickling the tips of my
toes like a mouse's whiskers.
The flowers, now awoken from a long winter sleep,
have burst out like the colours of the rainbow.
I imagine the field mice scuttling along inside the
bramble bushes as if preparing for a secret picnic.

The sun fades away now like the clouds have taken over and heavy raindrops beat against the greenhouse glass which sounds like a marching parade.
I rush inside now looking out onto my spring garden.

Esme Mitchell (9)
Longridge Towers School, Berwick-Upon-Tweed

The Disagreement Of The Ferocious Three

The T-rex, giganotosaurus and spinosaurus, a totally fearsome three,
Were walking through the lush forest and stopped beside a tree.
Their voices were loud and shouting, an argument was brewing,
They just could not agree on who was the biggest of the Ferocious Three.

T-Rex said, "I am king of the dinosaurs, although my arms might be small."
Spinosaurus said, "I am tall, T-Rex, but you, my friend, are as small as a baseball."
Giganotosaurus said, "No, I am the tallest and if you disagree, I will maul you all."

Suddenly the tree started to wobble and unpleasantly shake,
It started to move, a voice could be heard from way above the tree.

A long neck of sorts could be seen, an argentinosaurus was looking down with glee. "None of you are the biggest," he said. "That prize belongs to me!"

Jake Stephens (10)

Longridge Towers School, Berwick-Upon-Tweed

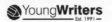
Seasons

Spring is such a lovely time
Flowers are beginning to grow
The bleating lamb is a sign
That it is time to sow.

The combine is harvesting crop
Which has been growing right through the year
You can smell the barbecue next door having corn
on the cob
And hear the cap opening on a cold beer.

The golden leaves fall off the trees
A sign that autumn has come
The leaves dance in the chilly breeze
Which makes my fingers and toes go numb.

Winter is when Jack Frost comes out to play
The north wind has its time to blow
We wait and wait for Christmas Day
And hopefully lots of snow.

Tom Parmenter (10)
Longridge Towers School, Berwick-Upon-Tweed

What Am I?

I have a body,
But no arms or legs,
I have a stem,
But no leaves or petals,
I can be made from any material,
And I bathe in a bubble bath after work.

I slumber beside my extended family,
I lie still until I am needed,
I require assistance to move,
But I can carry other materials,
And I can help you if you're ill.

My work can be boiling hot or icy cold,
I help deliver goods to where they are needed,
I can measure,
But I don't need a ruler or scales,
And I can never work alone.

What am I?

Answer: I am a spoon!

Erin Macfarlane (10)
Longridge Towers School, Berwick-Upon-Tweed

The Haunted House

The house I live in,
Where the temperature stays the same,
Always cold and never hot,
And uninvited vampires stand at your door.

The curtains dance,
And the wind plays the flute,
My dog whines non-stop
And a smell of regret covers the rooms.

The house I live in,
Where the bedsheets are spiderwebs
And the walls are reinforced with tears
With all the doors sealed.

The house is as dark as a bat flying in the night sky
And inside all hope is lost
Everyone can get in but not out
The house where the light does not shine
The house I live in.

Lukas Rowlands (10)
Longridge Towers School, Berwick-Upon-Tweed

The Cloudy Skies

I think the clouds in the sky
Changing shapes up so high
They matter to me quite a lot
I see them with my eye

I once saw a flock of sheep
I saw them flying by
They made me go into a deep sleep
I dreamt of a nice time

And then I saw a toucan
Searching the clouds for fish
It kept on looking and looking
But only found a dish

I also saw a penguin
Powering through the air
They think they know penguins can't fly
This one is willing to dare.

Giles Gibb (9)
Longridge Towers School, Berwick-Upon-Tweed

The Clouds

The clouds whisper gently to me
Through the howling wind
Touching the tip of my tongue.

The clouds cry
As their tears touch the ground
Like a mouse tiptoeing quietly along the path.

The clouds cast shadows
Constantly moving as if
Ants were running across the road.

The clouds bounce off each other
Like children playing tag
Bouncing off each other with their hands.

Harry Cairns (10)

Longridge Towers School, Berwick-Upon-Tweed

My Evening

I was happily talking to my cousin
I really wanted to play Fortnite
Everything was set up
But I had to do this learning log tonight.

My brother and dad asked me to shoot with them
I really wanted to hit a target too
They all went outside
But I had some poem writing to do.

I nearly finished my poem
I really wanted to stop
But I had to go to bed
My evening was a big flop!

Oliver van Boeckel van Rumpt (10)
Longridge Towers School, Berwick-Upon-Tweed

Seeds Of Change

Out in the fields there's work that needs to be done
Time to change the fields from green into brown

Ploughing the land, getting rid of the weeds
Ready to sow with new blooming seeds

Now we need rain followed by sun
Watch the seeds grow and pop out the ground

Every day the crops grow taller
Not long now till the combine goes over!

Charlie Baird (10)
Longridge Towers School, Berwick-Upon-Tweed

Tiggy

I ride a pony called Tiggy,
She is very fast,
She loves to gallop
And she is never last.

She loves to go on a hack,
Then she is full of spring,
She is always ready to go
And she makes my heart sing.

Gallop, gallop,
What a sound!
I feel more happy in the saddle
Than with my feet on the ground!

Paulien Wagner (9)
Longridge Towers School, Berwick-Upon-Tweed

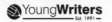
The Teacup

I like my tea hot and strong
"Hurry up!" says Mum
"Put the kettle on."

The teacups rattle
"I hope it's me!" says Mum's favourite cup
"Oh no, not me," says cup number three.

But the cup that Mum wants so much
Is the coronation cup
The kids love so much!

Ihsan Saygilier (10)
Longridge Towers School, Berwick-Upon-Tweed

My Little Red Panda

Oh my little red panda
You went for a little gander
Along a rocky track
As your eyes are so black

Oh my little red panda
Off for a little gander
And you met a friendly frog
In a giant bog

Oh my little red panda
With a friend called Amanda
She is a dog
Who chased the friendly frog.

Maisie Wilson (10)
Longridge Towers School, Berwick-Upon-Tweed

Trains

Thundering and clattering,
Thousands of trains,
Go this way and that,
All over the plains.

Hills and mountains,
Thousands of rivers,
Through towns and villages,
All over in a flicker.

Passengers and cargo,
Thousands of stations,
Rushing here and there,
All over the nation.

Rocco Lindsay (10)
Longridge Towers School, Berwick-Upon-Tweed

My Ski Trip

The day before skiing,
I get an excited feeling,
To be climbing high,
And feeling the skiing vibe.

The crunch of the snow,
The nip on my nose,
Clicking into my boots...
"Come on, let's go!"

Steaming hot chocolate,
Marshmallow and cream,
Yummy!

Poppy Douglas (10)
Longridge Towers School, Berwick-Upon-Tweed

The Dirt Bike Dream

I love riding my dirt bike
Over the jumps
High so high
Just like I could fly

I love the roar
Of the engine
In my ear
And it shakes my spine with fear

Doing skids is much more fun
Than making circles
When I ride
I could almost glide.

Harvey Mcdonald (10)
Longridge Towers School, Berwick-Upon-Tweed

Tat The Cat

Once there was a cat called Tat,
She likes to chat
And sit on mats.

When Tat eats rats
She spits and spats,
Tat is a big brat.

She plays the instruments this way and that,
But all she does is rat-a-tat-tat,
Then Pat gets angry and gnats at Tat.

Wren Pearson (10)
Longridge Towers School, Berwick-Upon-Tweed

My Boy

Funny long ears,
Beautiful brown eyes,
Raises his paw,
Almost looks wise,
A strange, little, dark nose,
A kind, loving critter,
Always around and
Always near.

Ruby Richardson (10)
Longridge Towers School, Berwick-Upon-Tweed

My Friend Nature

Nature has always been my friend,
Since I was the littlest girl.
I have always watched the changes happen,
It makes my mind start to swirl.
Yesterday, a blackbird built its nest, selecting
different twigs.
Our garden providing all it needed as it chose its
different sprigs.
It scurried them away, into our tree,
Time to rest its legs.
Surely over the next few weeks,
It will be filled with blackbird eggs.

Martha Francis (8)

Milldene Primary School, Tiptree

Summertime

On summer mornings I see the bold, beautiful sun
Beaming through my window like a light in my
face.
As I open my curtain and see the tiny vegetables
popping up
I'm filled with happiness and feel relaxed and full
of joy.

On the hottest days I go to the magical and
glorious beach
And I see the water covering the sand like a warm
blanket.
When I buy ice cream, I see people's ice cream
melting like snow in the sun.

In afternoons whilst I swing as high as The Shard
I hear the barbecue sizzling and it always smells
delicious.
When it's really hot I go to the ice cube dispenser
and make a cold drink.

My sister and I love swimming, so we get the paddling pool out and we race around like fools.

We love summertime!

Benjamin Lucas (8)
Milldene Primary School, Tiptree

The Fearless Bob

Cats, cats
Everywhere
What should I do?
They're everywhere
But
The greatest of them all
Is Bob
With his hazel eyes
Sharp fangs
And nibbled ears
His radar eyes search the night sky
For a tasty meal
His razor-sharp fangs crunch on the bones
He comes in to rest
That's my pet cat.

Lily Bonnyhood (8)
Milldene Primary School, Tiptree

Stock Car

S kegness Raceway is the best
T aking corners like the rest
O val tracks are quite a test
C ome in first you win the prize
K eep on going around the track

C rash and you are at the back
A aron is my favourite
R acing fast and winning trophies.

Kieran Grimwade (8)
Milldene Primary School, Tiptree

Me

P urple is my favourite colour
H ow much I love to be outside is amazing
O h don't let me, how much I love koalas
E very rose I see I love to smell
B ees flying above my head
E very flower I smell gives me joy.

Phoebe Herman (7)
Milldene Primary School, Tiptree

My Dog Brandy

My dog Brandy is very crazy
Whenever he meets Maisie he's very lazy

Brandy is sandy and he likes the beach
But for some reason he doesn't like the sea

I love my dog Brandy.

Rosie Terry (8)
Milldene Primary School, Tiptree

Friends

Me and Isla play all day
Skipping and saying hooray
It was night
We said wake up
Bright in the morning light
It was morning
Now the trees were moving
And the bees were snoozing.

Hallie Coney (8)
Milldene Primary School, Tiptree

All The Reasons I Love My Family

I love my family
My mum is lovely
My daddy is very strong
Me and my brother fight a lot
But he is the best brother
Together we make a team
And I love my family!

Yaqub Al-Mahfuz (8)

Milldene Primary School, Tiptree

Roblox

R oblox is a game to play

O nly for one hour

B ig boys only

L oud cars

O range cars drive

E **X** ploding.

Max Fletcher (8)

Milldene Primary School, Tiptree

Capybara

C apybara fur is fuzzy but soft
A lways growing their teeth continuously
P urring loudly to family members
Y oung pups swimming with their mums
B ig cats are their predators
A dult capybaras grow to 106-134cm
R eddish brown fur all over their bodies
A magnificent creature.

Lydia Minshull (8)

St Bernard's RC Primary School, Ellesmere Port

Nature

N ature is beauty

A lways growing leaves and flowers everywhere

T rees give us life

U nusual creatures wander around this beautiful place

R ainbow shining brightly in the sky

E verywhere we look we can see nature.

Sadie Whitfield (9)
St Bernard's RC Primary School, Ellesmere Port

Summer Sun

S un is shining down on the children
U nder the tree they find some shade
M um is in the kitchen making ice cream
M um asked if we wanted some
E xcited, we rushed to the kitchen
R eady to eat the yummy ice cream.

Brooke Fairweather-Barry (8)
St Bernard's RC Primary School, Ellesmere Port

Friends

F riends are always there for you
R eady to play every day
I love my friends
E ven when we argue
N ever snacks they share
D efinitely make you feel happy
S miling at each other.

Sofia Perkins (9)
St Bernard's RC Primary School, Ellesmere Port

Friend

F riends forever

R unning together when we're excited

I nstantly helping when someone falls over

E very time being kind and caring

N ever arguing

D ancing and laughing all day long.

Emilia Mae Fitzgerald (9)

St Bernard's RC Primary School, Ellesmere Port

My Family

F un times together
A lways laughing at big brother's jokes
M um cooking delicious food
I love my family
L oving everyone the same
Y our family is more important than money.

Texas Sweeney (9)
St Bernard's RC Primary School, Ellesmere Port

Your Family Loves You

F antastic people
A person that you can talk to
M akes you comfortable
I s a group who likes you for you
L oves you for who you are
Y our family are perfect.

Esmai Cooper (9)
St Bernard's RC Primary School, Ellesmere Port

Midnight Monsters

M agicians that appear in the sky.

I n the cupboard eating pie.

D ownstairs or upstairs, they're always there

N ight-time or daytime, do you know they're there?

I magine his glare, if you dare

G ateaux is what they eat, probably under a tree!

H ave you ever watched Monsters, Inc.?

T ime to go to the bathroom, but I wouldn't when they are there

M uch too skinny or maybe fat, who cares we've all seen that!

O n the table lies your lunch, then they come and eat it up!

N ow then, stay still as they pierce your ears with a drill

S ometimes they're naughty just like you

T errible, that's not true

E ven if you need the loo they won't let you

R ude, who are you talking to?

S ettle down, now this whole poem wasn't true!

Ellie Garrod (9)
St Mary's CE Primary School, Sheffield

124

I Love Brownies

I love brownies, I love brownies by the sea

L ike most brownie lovers, I even eat on my bike

O h brownie, this brownie is not tat

V acuum crumbs off the floor, waiting to consume some more

E veryone likes brownies, why wouldn't they?

B rownies are the best

R ight, that's true

O h I hope you love brownies too

W hen I had my first

N ibble, I gave a little giggle

I love brownies and I hope you do too

E veryone

S hould like them, I hope you do too.

Faith Masaba-Kituyi (9)
St Mary's CE Primary School, Sheffield

Beautiful

B eing kind isn't hard, I believe I can do it if I always try because it is easy to be kind.

E veryone can be kind when they try new things!

A nyone can do anything if they try.

U plifting my friends keeps me happy.

T ears are good things, they show your emotions!

I t's alright if you have no friends, the way you get some is by respecting them

F abulous people are fabulous, you're one of them!

U nited Kingdom is my favourite place

L oving people is a good thing I do!

Tia Shanice Stacey Thompson (8)

St Mary's CE Primary School, Sheffield

The Jet

T ime has passed since I, the great inventor, created jet number 4

H aving it was quite a bore

E ven though it had fire-breathing boosters, I think I would have preferred a plain brown rooster

J umping cogs and churning springs, a beautiful rainbow that's what I'd use

E ven though it was like a golf course, I think I would have preferred a smelly horse!

T he wishing star asked me, it wanted to know, why oh why did you hate the jet so?

Connie Ovenden (8)

St Mary's CE Primary School, Sheffield

If I Ruled The World...

If I ruled the world...
I would let every item be free
And let the world follow me.

If I ruled the world...
I would make everyone be nice
And not eat mice.

If I ruled the world...
I would help people learn
And earn success.

If I ruled the world...
I would help people do what they want to do
And have food.

If I ruled the world...
I would help people's dreams come true
And help them through.

Sally Bola (9)
St Mary's CE Primary School, Sheffield

Why I Love Animals

Animals are kind
Like your best friend forever
That's why I love animals

Animals are adorable
And loyal like your heart
That's why I love animals

Animals are protective and sometimes fearsome
Animals hunt like Vikings
That's why I love animals

Animals are mostly playful and active
And sleepy and stubborn
That's why I love animals.

Venuhya Reddy Neelam (9)
St Mary's CE Primary School, Sheffield

Hobbies

Hobbies just to name a few,
Ballet, gymnastics and ice skating too,
These are the things I like to do.
Ice skating is cold but warm when you move,
Gliding on the ice that's nice and smooth,
With class and grace is how I groove,
Tricks from ballet I sometimes use,
Imagining I'm alone in the room.
Flexible like a gymnast too.
These are my hobbies just to name a few.

Lillie-Lovélle Melville (9)

St Mary's CE Primary School, Sheffield

All About Me

A bdwadood is my name

B anana is my favourite fruit

D ark doesn't scare me

W ater is good for me because it is healthy

A utomatic car is my dream car

D ear Mother cares for me, I will always appreciate her

O range is my second-best fruit

O n the day when we go to the park I am always excited

D oing crafts sometimes.

Abdwadood Qasim (9)

St Mary's CE Primary School, Sheffield

Dominic

D ora is a beautiful German shepherd

O wned by me and my family

M inecraft, Zelda, Ring Fit Adventure, Geometry Dash and Stray

I love all these games

N ow my favourite football team are in the Premier League

I love running, speed, volcanoes, gaming and football

C andy and Sweetie are the best guinea pigs ever; I love my pets.

Dominic Gregory (9)

St Mary's CE Primary School, Sheffield

Juliette Animal Lover

J uliette loves animals

U nmistakeable as it is

L oves rabbits, dogs and even koala bears

I f one more species is to become extinct - disaster

E ven if it were elephants she would not be happy

T all giraffe, she likes them all

T ells them that it doesn't matter if they're small

E very animal deserves love.

Juliette Hart (9)

St Mary's CE Primary School, Sheffield

Elephants

E lephants are funny
L oveable and small
E lephants are big
P retty elephants are tall
H appy elephants
A mazing elephants
N avigate their troops
T ravelling for miles they walk to find food.

Grace Woods (8)
St Mary's CE Primary School, Sheffield

All About Me

I nterested in football

A Nintendo Switch in hand
M y favourite food is pizza

T aking walks with my family
O n my way to number 10 (age)
M y family is Mum, Dad, my sister and me.

Tom Mason (9)
St Mary's CE Primary School, Sheffield

My Family

F un is my family
A nd I love them very much
M y family are my biggest fans
I don't know what I would do without them
L ife is better with them around
Y ou should come and meet them.

Elsie Gibbins (9)
St Mary's CE Primary School, Sheffield

Books

B ooks are very important
O pen a book and knowledge will follow
O nly key to becoming an intelligent person
K nowledge means books
S uccess is your way if you read books regularly.

Aarav Sonwal (9)
St Mary's CE Primary School, Sheffield

Something Yummy

I am yummy but not a bunny
I go in your tummy but I'm not so funny
Most people love me
But if you have too much of me
I'm not so lovely
I am cold and my colours are quite bold.
What am I?

Mila Goodwin (9)

St Mary's CE Primary School, Sheffield

Beautiful, Lovely Wave

W aves are gorgeous and splendid
A t sunset the waves are even more beautiful
V oice of the birds chirping goes with the waves
E very night the sunset brings the waves up.

Nur Amna Shahirzaman (9)
St Mary's CE Primary School, Sheffield

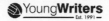

About Me

L ovely and full of joy
U nique and unpredictable like a child's toy
K ind with a gentle touch
A dventurous, always up for so much.

Luka Slavica (9)
St Mary's CE Primary School, Sheffield

Bonfire Night

Bonfire bright at midnight
Fire crackling in the
Flattering night
As winter air begins to
Rise
The summer breeze tries to
Fight back.

Nuri Bennaser (9)
St Mary's CE Primary School, Sheffield

Pies In The Sky

A lovely pie in the sky,
All crunchy and gooey,
All tasty and chewy.
Cut it with a knife and have some fun,
I love pie, what a great pun!
A lovely pie in the sky,
All fancy and mushy,
All great and smooshy.
With chicken and gravy
And turkey and mushroom.
A gravy explosion, it goes boom!
What a lovely pie in the sky,
I love it so much I feel like a fly!
A lovely pie in the sky,
With beef and onion,
With chips and peas,
I almost forgot, with some cheese!
What a lovely pie in the sky,
All crunchy and gooey,
All tasty and chewy.
Yeah, I love pie, do you like pie?

Yeah, I like pie, do you like pie?
Yeah, I love pie, you do like pie!
You can have it with chips and peas
And some beef, please
With cheese and onion,
With gravy and turkey.

Tommy Corbett-Hardiman (9)
White Hall Academy, Clacton-On-Sea

Elements

Flickering, dancing, hot to the touch,
This element can bring us so very much,
Respect is needed with this force of nature,
Fire is the element, one of four, the rest to come later.
Rivers, lakes, ponds, oceans and seas,
When left in the cold it could freeze,
This element can cause floods and devastation,
Water is the element which is the source of all life's foundation.
Flowers, mud, stone and grass,
Also sand which can make glass,
In this element plants and trees sprout,
Earth is the element I'm talking about.
Causing tornadoes and hurricanes,
In this element two things fly, those are birds and planes,
It mainly blows east or west,
This is air as you probably guessed.
Here are the elements of water, fire, earth and air,
I hope you enjoyed this, now remember, take care.

Oliver Millar (9)
White Hall Academy, Clacton-On-Sea

The Month Of May

T ime for May, summer's almost here
H ow is it already nearly half the year?
E ven the bluebells have come out to say hello

M ornings are lighter
O ff to school in summer dresses
N ights are lighter too
T ime off school with bank holidays
H alf term too

O h the sea breeze reminds us it's still spring
F antasising about holidays yet to come

M any days in the garden tidying and playing
A king's coronation in 2023
Y ay for May and the hopes of summer it brings!

Phoebe Thurgood (9)
White Hall Academy, Clacton-On-Sea

My Journey In Primary School

On my first day I was very nervous, I walked in all
alone
But I knew my parents were just on the other side
of the phone.
I made lots of friends, now we're happy as can be,
And my teachers were always happy with me.
I do have a favourite teacher but I mustn't say,
But if I told her it would make her day.
I'll soon be doing my SATs which will show me my
way
But I'll be sad on my very last day.
So goodbye, White Hall, thank you for having me,
I'm off to high school, just watch me and see.

Sophie Chapman (11)

White Hall Academy, Clacton-On-Sea

Blue Whales

In the deep blue sea where the waves roll free
Lives a creature so grand
A beauty of the ocean and once the land
The blue whale is its name
A gentle giant in the ocean blue
Its body is huge and strong
And also very long
The water is where it swims
Their voices echoing as they sing
They eat up to four tonnes of krill!
It gives them such a thrill!
The blue whale's heart is as big as a car!
They travel just as far!
In the beautiful blue sea
They swim in pods, they are family!

Isabella Kitchener (7)
White Hall Academy, Clacton-On-Sea

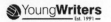

The Journey

The world is vast
The world is wide
So many places to explore and hide
From busy streets to the countryside
There's always something new to find
The sun rises and the sun sets
A new day comes with no regrets
The world keeps turning, without rest
And we keep moving, doing our best
So let's take a moment to appreciate
All the beauty in the world, both big and great
From the smallest flowers to the grandest state
This world is ours, let's celebrate!

Lewis Hogg (11)
White Hall Academy, Clacton-On-Sea

The Pea And The Crow

There was a pea who was neat and clean.
There was a crow who wore a pretty pink bow.
Whilst the pea was in the glistening white snow
In the snow she lay and dreamt of not being able
to age.
She didn't want to get old,
Though she wanted to meet the wise old crow.
Summer was getting closer,
As she sat writing under the lamppost.
She saw glimpses of the wise old crow,
Flying towards the sweet little pea,
And she smiled as she knew she was going to be
free.

Serenna Ord (9)
White Hall Academy, Clacton-On-Sea

Summer

I drank my lemonade as it was a nice summer day.
The warm wind whispered on me while wobbling
my ice cream.
I relaxed on the comfy hammock with a very full
stomach.
The golden bright sun smiled at me while I drank
my lemonade.
The light breeze of the wind made the trees sway.
I sighed loudly at the clouds above me.
They ran left and right like cats and dogs starting
a fight.
Summer is here, the end is not near,
Hard time for waiting, this is not about
participating.

Jessica Ajayi-Obe (10)
White Hall Academy, Clacton-On-Sea

Goodbye White Hall

I'm onto my next adventure,
I'll never forget the memories, friends and fun that
I had there.
Let's all give a cheer for Miss Harvey and Mrs
Kerry,
Who have helped us through this very hard year.
I'm very sad to be leaving and scared of what's
ahead,
You have taught me life skills so I know I can do it.
Teachers have taught me how to spell and read.
Goodbye, White Hall, I am off to my big school,
I'm going to miss you all but never forget.

Tiahna-Rose White (11)

White Hall Academy, Clacton-On-Sea

Best Buddies

Oh, dear Peter,
To me, you are like a brother.
Your love is that of a mother.
Given a chance, I would choose you as my father.
If I lost you in the wilderness I would wander.
I can't imagine a life far from each other.
Without you, I would live like a squatter.
I will do anything to make sure we are together.
Let's have our lunch on a silver platter.
The way you're dressed, you look like a baker.
You are my friend, my greatest achiever.

Jacob Bondo (11)
White Hall Academy, Clacton-On-Sea

Friendship

Friendship is a bond that cannot be broken,
A connection that is never spoken.

It's a feeling of trust and loyalty,
A love that is pure and full of royalty.

Friends are there through thick and thin,
A support system that's always within.

They laugh with you and wipe your tears,
And help you conquer all your fears.

Friends share secrets and inside jokes,
And always know when you're feeling broke.

Ella Ryan-Smith (10)
White Hall Academy, Clacton-On-Sea

My Time At White Hall

My time at White Hall has been a blast,
Although sometimes it can be daft.
I've made fabulous friends,
As I grow they continue to ascend.
Learning new things to help me on my way,
I hope these things never go away.
As my time at primary school comes to a finish,
I'll never forget where it all began or let my
memories diminish.
Thank you, White Hall, time for me to spread my
wings and fly,
I'm going to reach for the sky.

Millie Crouch (10)
White Hall Academy, Clacton-On-Sea

Goodbye White Hall Academy

White Hall is fun when you make friends
But sad when it comes to an end.
Saying goodbye to the teachers we know so well.
They taught us to learn and spell.
They taught us so much.
I hope we still keep in touch.
I've been here for six years
But when I think of leaving all I have is tears.
Now that I have to say goodbye I am really sad.
Don't worry, I won't forget the times we had.

Goodbye, White Hall.

Amelie-Rose McKinnon (11)
White Hall Academy, Clacton-On-Sea

I Love Cars

I Love Cars

I like the vibrant colours of cars

L oads of different cars

O nly sometimes they are loud

V auxhall is a very cool car, the logo looks like a bird

E ventually in the future they might make flying cars

C ars are sometimes fast and sometimes slow

A ll of the cars are different

R arely you see green, purple or pink cars

S oon I will have my own car.

Summer Rollings (10)
White Hall Academy, Clacton-On-Sea

The Sandy Beach

The beach is a place where the sea meets the land,
Where the waves crash upon the shore,
And the sun warms the sand.

It's a place where we go to escape the daily chase,
And look around for a jellyfish case.
With the salty breeze blowing through our hair,
And the sound of the waves filling the air.

We can build sandcastles and fly kites in the sky,
Or simply lie back and watch the world go by.

Gracie Hodgson (10)
White Hall Academy, Clacton-On-Sea

The Clever Dog Treva

My dog Treva is ever so clever
He can even predict the weather
If it's rain or snow
He's bound to know
He's so clever they call him Professor Treva
He has a tattoo and does kung fu
He doesn't have time to argue with cats
Instead, he does maths and SATs
He doesn't wanna go on a long walk
Instead, he tries to learn how to talk
He's the most clever dog ever
My dog Treva!

Niamh Allen (9)
White Hall Academy, Clacton-On-Sea

Cat In The Hat

Hello, I am a cat in a hat!
I like you to give me a pat because I am a friendly cat!
I am crazy and a bit zany and brainy
And when it is rainy I'm quite crazy.
As Sally and Nick sat at home
As their mother was at work
Nick was taking the Mick out of Sally!
Until our friendly cat in the hat came and began to shout,
"Hi, boys and girls,
I'm here to make you laugh like a giraffe!"

Miya Park (10)
White Hall Academy, Clacton-On-Sea

The Croaky Frog

There once was a frog
Who lived in a bog
It ran down the street
Until it heard a beat
The beat of a thumb
Banging in a drum
One day he got lost
On the road he crossed
"Oh no," said the frog
Who lived in a bog
There was no street
There was no beat
Only a dog
Sat on a log.

Kenzie Sadd (8)
White Hall Academy, Clacton-On-Sea

The Fun Of My Pet Dog

The fun of my pet dog is endless, is it not?
Big or small, he is fun no matter what.
He likes to run around.
He has strong muscles
So he can tug all of us around.
Thor has a slobbery tongue to slobber on me with.
Even though he is a bully
He is so gentle with me and my family.

TJ Wiegand (11)
White Hall Academy, Clacton-On-Sea

Animals

A nimals are amazing friends
N aughty when they are babies
I tchy if they have fleas
M ajestic beasts rule the forests
A crobatic species live in the jungle
L oyal friends until the end
S pecial in their own way.

Jai Moore-O'neill (7)

White Hall Academy, Clacton-On-Sea

Feathers

Hope is like feathers
It comes and goes
Feathers appear when angels appear
They are strong with purpose but light at heart
These are like angel wings
Wings can fly as high as can be
What a wonderful place up there
Feathers are everywhere.

Kasey Carlisle (9)
White Hall Academy, Clacton-On-Sea

Oh Mr Monkey

Oh Mr Monkey, you are so funky swinging through
the trees,
Your hands are hairy, not all that scary,
Your favourite fruit is cherry,
You're very merry,
You're only scared of Kerry!
Oh Mr Monkey, I love you.

James Campbell (8)
White Hall Academy, Clacton-On-Sea

The Cat And The Dog

The cat and the dog had a frog
That was in the fog
And the cat with a hat
And a bat was on the mat
With the dog called Pat.
The frog in the fog
Found the dog on the mat
With the cat.

Lenny McDonagh (7)
White Hall Academy, Clacton-On-Sea

Fat Cat

Once there was a cat
Who was so fat
That he couldn't even lie down.
He had a hat
He wore it and slipped
Then his bottom ripped
And its owner threw up
Straight into his new cup.

Emmanuel Siby (8)
White Hall Academy, Clacton-On-Sea

Future

In the future, I'd like to see my idols
And reunite with family and friends
Because after I leave White Hall
I won't see most of my friends
Because they are going to a different school.

Ethan Dobbs (10)
White Hall Academy, Clacton-On-Sea

My Crazy Cat

My crazy cat was big and fat
That lay on a mat with a big, fat, stinky, old street rat
There was a cat with a stinky old mat
That sat with a rat
That sat on a stinky old mat.

Myah Harrington (8)
White Hall Academy, Clacton-On-Sea

Aston The Great

A is for awesome boy
S is for super good mind
T is for terrific writer
O is for outstanding creator
N is for not a quitter!

Aston Harris (8)
White Hall Academy, Clacton-On-Sea

What Am I?

I keep you dry not warm
I'm most useful in a storm
You can buy me anywhere
I keep rain off your hair
I'm not a coat nor a towel.
What am I...?

George Barnes (10)
White Hall Academy, Clacton-On-Sea

The Haunted House

The ticking of the clock,
The flashing of the lights,
The noises of the dogs,
The popping of the toaster
And all the sounds can be heard throughout the night!

Noah Shirra (9)

White Hall Academy, Clacton-On-Sea

Big Fat Rat

There was a big fat rat
Who got scared of a cat
And got trapped under a hat.
There was also a bat
Hiding under a mat
Wearing a funny hat.

Thea-Elizabeth Pobjoy (7)
White Hall Academy, Clacton-On-Sea

Cat And Bat

The cat was blind as a bat
Sat on the mat
Because it was fat
It met a wild bat
The bat called the cat a brat!

Caitlin Hearne (7)
White Hall Academy, Clacton-On-Sea

Dog On A Log

There was a dog
Sitting on a log
On a rock with a lock
Who hits a sock with a block
What a shock!

Sophia Dray (8)

White Hall Academy, Clacton-On-Sea

What Will You Be When You Grow Up?

What will you be when you grow up?
Will you be a firefighter putting out fires, maybe caused by lighters?
Or even a vet?
Let's hope they take care of your pet!

What will you be when you grow up?
Are your hopes to be climbing ropes?
I don't know if I could cope!
Or are your dreams to be making memes and streams as a YouTuber?

What will you be when you grow up?
Will you be a nurse carrying a special purse?
Would you risk the blood and worry? I couldn't think of anything worse!

Or are you destined to be a teacher, having a lot of special features:
Patience, intelligence and shaping the minds of young creatures!

What will you be when you grow up?

Neve Powell (10)
Whitleigh Community Primary School, Whitleigh

The Beautiful Star

As the discoid hot sun glances at the goliath
That is flying in the wind
The blimp rises, you see a blue, clear waterfall.
Rare, divine petals like toys in the white fluffy
clouds,
O'er the mountaintops the goliath flies like a hawk
in the skies.

Gas balloons fly in the skies like a flock of geese,
When the balloon gets higher it feels like climbing
the tallest mountain on earth, Mount Everest,
It flies in the wind like a lady's skirt.
Swaying in the balloon goes side to side.
The Milky Way clouds move with them.

The balloon is like a football being booted into the
sky,
As they fly higher you see rainbow balloons like
cotton candy clouds stay with them,
The spangly star glows in the moonlight.

Hung in the sky the beautiful star in the sky shines.
Waves in the wind.

Brooke H (11)
Winsford High Street CP School, Winsford

Flying Through The Air

Bright gold suns beaming onto the floating goliath,
Gliding through the basest clouds almost the
colossal mountains,
Below emerald green grass danced in fields,
Marching above crystal, translucent streams.

Soaring o'er misty meadow patched together by a
thread of hedgerows,
Floating o'er treacherous linns being clutched in
place by rose skies,
Bending boughs o'erhang the enormous cliffs,
The oval-shaped ball being kicked through the sky.

Large green leaves crash into the deep dells,
The towering mountains surround great valleys,
The giant lollipop glides through the misty
meadows,
The colossal gasbag flutters through the
candyfloss.

The zephyr blows the enormous air ball,
A candyfloss cloud emerging from the abyss.

Logan Powell (11)
Winsford High Street CP School, Winsford

Up In The Air

Drifting in the atmosphere flew a balloon,
The gliding eagle pierced through the puffy clouds,
Clear blue river danced as their king flew,
As the balloon stared amber colour appeared.

Across the pink, glossy sky stood a tree,
Like Jack and the beanstalk stand sweet people,
The balloon was a sparkly star at night,
The floating goliath took off with height.

Large colourful balloon delve over the grass,
Spring across like a frog jumping over its lake,
Looking small, the balloon towers like a beast,
Dancing like friends they all seem to care.

Their football deflates as the stars come out,
The balloon o'hung the trees as it popped.

Aaron Mcgee (11)
Winsford High Street CP School, Winsford

Dancing In The Wind

Dancing among the hazy morning clouds,
The fearsome giant scopes the land while up high,
Stomps through the clouds like a king in its crown,
Emerald green grass glares as people start to
stare.

Dancing in the wind, balloons start to sing,
Puzzling mountains sit on the beautiful horizon,
Jumping in the sky, balloons start to fly,
Footballs in the sky while cars start to drive.

Looking up at the glistening sunset,
The huge, warm balloon starts to take flight,
Like a shooting star whizzing in the air,
The spangled star lights the way to the sky.

All balloons glide like a flock of white geese,
Ancient old baskets as warm as a blast.

Mason P (11)
Winsford High Street CP School, Winsford

A Spring Day

Rising gently with care,
The small patchwork balloon drifts off gliding
through the air,
Setting off on an expedition.

Hovering below clouds,
Ribbons of water run through valleys,
Ending at a fascinating waterfall.

Trees decorate forests with speckles of variegated
hues,
Fields of bright daffodils and marble moth orchids
linger,
Embracing the minimal sunlight.

Waves crash on sloped, rocky edges of cliffs,
As the sun sets - colliding with the ocean,
Leaving only a celestial view of dazzling stars and
a shining moon.

At last, the day has ended and it may now rest,
As for another spring day shall return again.

Daniella Kosina (11)
Winsford High Street CP School, Winsford

The Hot Air Balloon

The skyscrapers leapt across the sunrise,
With glorious meadows all around us.
There is beautiful gliding here,
With blooming blossoms dancing in the breeze.

Dancing among the hazy morning clouds,
With colourful butterflies all around.
It cast its gaze across the patchwork fields,
Green, yellow, stitched together by hedgerow
thread.

The beaming sun has left some shade over there,
Whilst it was shining as it had a fan in front of it.
The sun loves to be the horizon here,
Over the glossy sea early in the morning light.

The poor spring flowers are starting to die,
Bye spring, my best friend, I will see you next year.

Grace Pearson (11)
Winsford High Street CP School, Winsford

A Balloon's Journey In The Sky

As it began its journey in the air,
There were many things the balloons could see,
Down the sovereign eye of the sun glared,
As the golden face glared, it glared with glee.

Dancing amidst the misty morning clouds,
The balloons were birds drifting in the sky,
They flew above the bending blue rivers,
And they passed the green, grassy mountain tops.

They looked down at the beryl waterfalls,
Which were leading into the crystal streams,
The painted circular birds could almost stroke the clouds,
And had a marvellous view of the deep dells.

They floated atop the emerald meads,
As the balloons rose, they seemed to be smaller.

Jenson L (11)
Winsford High Street CP School, Winsford

Flying Through The Air

Elegant rose skies surround bright balloons,
Pearly clouds disco like aerialists,
Jade grass whips and whirls in the freshly
humidified air,
Mini birds chirp their favourite song loudly.

The sun blast reflects off the balloon,
Revolving off the high-top mountains,
Hollow trees get jabbed by the freezing rain,
The sound is like ladies' skirts brushing the grass.

People watch it like it's a cinema,
Black and yellow bees run around the huge globe,
Pale streams with heavenly alchemy,
Batting the bright, colourful flower abodes.

The sun lies on top of the great sphere,
An exquisite rainbow comes gradually.

Will T (11)
Winsford High Street CP School, Winsford

Balloon Through A Kingdom

A colossal balloon flew through the blue,
Going through valleys, mountains and even more,
The giant was a paintbrush that made dew,
Flying past a furious bear with claws.

The flying soul is just an owl at night,
Viewing steady flowing water was a thrill,
It could observe creatures having to write,
Being up in the strange sky was a chill.

It was such a nice day to fly outside,
Facing some white rabbits running from prey,
Looking at the scenic sight turned the tide,
The animal kingdom had blessed the day.

At the start, fauna screeched welcome, crying.
Finally, they were glum, then weeped goodbye.

Dylan Sandland (11)
Winsford High Street CP School, Winsford

The Hot Air Balloon

The colossal rays of colour awoke,
Painting the landscape a spectrum of colour.
It can see factories producing smoke
And the bright moon getting a lot duller.

The gleaming sun getting awfully bright,
Its eyes set upon the gleaming blue lake.
Oh, our beautiful nature, what a sight,
The long green grass swaying like a snake.

The happy birds singing brilliantly,
The triumphant trees holding their proud stance,
The sly, stealthy foxes sprinting swiftly,
The tall trees performing their daily dance.

But then sometimes the poison that nature brings,
It's full with many unfavourable things.

Ethan L W (11)
Winsford High Street CP School, Winsford

The Hot Air Balloon

Twirling among the hazy morning clouds,
A floating goliath whirled in the wind.
The celestial face of gold twinkled,
Peering above a land of morning dew.

Crashing waves reflecting gorgeous sunlight,
Meadows are met with blossoms of pink pearl.
Peaceful scenes woven with elegant beams,
Delicate scents lingered throughout nature.

It casts its gaze across patchwork fields,
Early sunrise brightens the dull with life.
Creating a patterned carpet within,
The sovereign eyes cast views of gold streams.

Suns of the world may stain the gloomy land,
Why does the spring have to leave us so soon?

Keira J (11)
Winsford High Street CP School, Winsford

The Hot Air Balloon

The skyscrapers leapt across the sunrise,
They watched animals wander on fields,
They see trees waving at them with a smile,
Reflective rivers crashed against the rocks.

Titans avoided each other with fear,
A celestial face lit up the site,
It kissed the green, vibrant meadows with care,
Gliding, pale streams with light and gold below.

The giant pirouetted gracefully,
Pink, white blossoms danced in the wind smoothly,
Garlands decorated the premises,
Flowers swayed in the zephyr lusciously.

Clouds cried turquoise rain and vicious wind blew,
As the night darkened, a severe storm grew.

Olivia G (11)
Winsford High Street CP School, Winsford

The Countryside

As the beautiful peach sunset appeared,
The colourful ball was kicked through peaks,
The lucid waterfall ran down the cliff,
Speedy cheetahs sprinted across the jade creeks.

Like Jack climbing up the beanstalk,
The balloon drifted into the twilight,
Deep dells full of crystal, translucent streams,
Twisted boughs o'erhung the colossal crag.

Misty meadows were run over by a stampede of
bulls,
A large vast of lush meads,
Like ducks, balloons created flying Vs,
Rainforests hung around the tracks of seeds.

People watched like it was a theatre,
They hoped to be in them one sunny day.

Theo James Ashford Williams (10)
Winsford High Street CP School, Winsford

The Hot Air Balloon

Glancing among the crystal river and the gazing
mountains is a shimmer below,
Manufactured by the celestial face that glimmers
triumphantly above the flying goliath.

The fields are yielding to the giants towering
above,
Whose gaze catches upon green and blue oceans
and
Meadows of beauty, gorgeous rivers
Streaming down the green mountains.

Leaves calmly falling down from the trees,
Glittering as they reach the ground,
Cows, sheep and pigs resting in their farms...
A candyfloss emerges to cover the sun...

Dark skies, rainy night, all animals hidden from
predators,
Beautiful skies disappearing.

Ethan Baddeley (11)
Winsford High Street CP School, Winsford

The Hot Air Balloon

Gracefully placed are ten multicoloured goliaths
twirling in the morning breeze
A heavenly face beamed on crashing waves
Skyscrapers twisting and turning with ease

Sovereign eye casts astonishing views
Over fields of yellow, green, filled with life
Animals are sunbathing in the zoos
People are strolling through the countryside

Towering waterfalls are collapsing
Down a mossy mountain that is jade green
With large nests of birds that are relaxing
Making sure that their small children are clean

Yet fields of green turn to fields of maroon
Why does spring have to leave the world so soon?

Grace Barlow (11)
Winsford High Street CP School, Winsford

Balloon In The Air

Coloured balloons treading through the sky,
Swaying air, balloon dancing like green grass,
Pink flowers swaying side to side,
Emerald grass on the rooftop of a cliff.

Dancing with the grey, hazy morning clouds,
The blue neon sky was beaming among us,
Bright-coloured birds peep through the floating
clouds,
Hovering clouds swaying as a bird.

The sparkly green grass lingered below us,
The football was pelted in the air,
In the crisp air a floating football was kicked,
A colossal balloon emerged in the sky.

The deep, dark sky shouted welcome,
It finally said its last goodbye.

Thomas Entwhistle (11)
Winsford High Street CP School, Winsford

The Hot Air Balloon's Journey

A crimson red globe leaping into action,
A soldier in training for lethal war,
Climbing, keeping an eye on all below,
Rocketing towards the beautiful sky,
Sailing across the undisturbed teal tide.

He will have surpassed the soaring cotton candy,
Floating island sailing on the blue sea,
Pointing down to the animals and grass,
Animals striding across the dry land.

A whole giant floating through the air,
The red balloon is starting to come down,
There are more special balloons here and there,
They're getting close, you can see a town,
Then it sadly lands, waiting for next time.

Jude Nicholson (11)
Winsford High Street CP School, Winsford

The Hot Air Balloon

Dancing among the towering mountains
The hovering titans pass humanity with glee,
Bright blue rivers are like water fountains,
But once they're off they are forever free,

The beaming sun which is shining so bright,
When the strong wind hits the sunflowers dance,
When autumn hits nature is out of sight,
But when the sun goes, flowers don't have a
chance,

Birds happily flap their wings,
Beneath the giant golden stream,
They chirp in front of the kings,
It feels like someone's dream,

The golden sunset makes the sky fade away,
Although it will be a beautiful day.

Logan Hitchmough (11)
Winsford High Street CP School, Winsford

The Hot Air Balloon

The floating gods scanning the land below
The forlorn clouds glide through the magic sky.
Waterfalls are baths going to overflow.
The vibrant birds are soaring through the clouds.

The celestial face forms a sunset,
Like golden paint being thrown on a wall.
Gilded sunset heating up the world below.
Airy clouds kissing the magical land.

Celestial face forming a sunset
Blooming blossoms inching over the lake,
Like leaning into the bright blue lagoon.
Daffodils sprouting in the scorching heat.

Tired sunset fading into the abyss,
Soaring titans floating o'er the surface.

Riley Cooper (11)
Winsford High Street CP School, Winsford

If I Were A Balloon

A white trophy cascade of water,
Diving into the deep plunge pool,
The dispersing clouds were low and dense,
Trickling down the floral stream was calm water.

The patchwork balloon whispered to the fluffy
clouds,
The sun cast its gorgeous, golden gaze across hazy
morning meadows full of daisies,
The glorious, glowing water sprinkled onto the soft
summer ground.

With the pretty, pink and purple sunset,
A sun arose with the delicate clouds,
The all-triumphant wind sang to blow the floating
goliath along,
A glorious morn welcomed golden daffodils.

In glee, the bright apple ascended.

Poppie W (11)
Winsford High Street CP School, Winsford

The Hot Air Balloon

The colossal giants wave their long arms,
Trying to reach the beautiful sunset.
The wind pushes it further from its grip.
Clouds cast shadows and cover-like blankets.

Floating skyscrapers dance through misty plains.
Peaceful landscapes kissed by a golden sun.
Gilding streams of warm, heavenly light.
Bouncing off the flowing river below.

Towering waterfalls cascade quickly,
Down the crystalised, glittery mountains,
Filled with nature so pure and natural.
A wonderful sensory reality.

Then the shadows cast even further.
Where have you gone my beloved summer?

Luca Heath (11)
Winsford High Street CP School, Winsford

The Hot Air Balloon

A colossal Air Force balloon,
Rising like a titan from its slumber.
Dancing amongst the dazzling sky light,
Illuminating the whole universe.

Hovering above the vulnerable land,
Casting shadows everywhere.
The crystal lake gleaming in the moonlight,
Glistening to the swift breeze.

The colour of plants blooming in the sunlight,
As towering trees lead the pack of nature.
The giant patchwork swaying with the clouds,
Glowing its eternal flame to light the way.

It seems the Air Force has found the right way,
After an exciting journey, let's call it a day.

Callum Abbiss (10)
Winsford High Street CP School, Winsford

I Wandered Lonely As A Balloon

Upon the gentle current of zephyr's path,
A goliath lay,
Colour on the balloon staineth,
Down below nature's play is displayed today.

The floating creation watched within never-ending
blue,
As nature paints her story,
With lush green and mountains nurs'd in dew,
A widening gaze shadow patchwork meadow
glory,
Stitched by fabric of the nature sew.

Soon, day rests as night awakes,
The spirit of night spread the glow,
While the celestial face partakes,
With skylight upon the Milky Way's show.

Down came the friends, back down to its creators.

Jenson Arundale (11)
Winsford High Street CP School, Winsford

The Hot Air Balloon

Dancing among the tasselled grass.
The flaming ball of gas awoke to start its lifelong dream.
It cast its long gaze across
The echoing beauty and soul of Niagara Falls.

Watching over as a guardian angel.
Making its way across the open skies.
It went to its ballet lesson, twirling around.
The overpowering elegance that is the titan's.

Which ruled the lively land below.
It rises to the clouds to play with
With the only rainbow.

They played for an hour over the delightful heavens,
It was time to go through the pearly clouds to continue its lifelong dream.

Piper Ode (11)
Winsford High Street CP School, Winsford

The Hot Air Balloon

Dancing among the fluffy clouds,
The flowy goliath floated across the land on a high up hill.
The frothy water dripping constantly
And marvellously glaring up at the sky full of curiosity.

The rumbling water plunged into a mossy lake full of fun and wonder.
The sun had its brown golden eyes staring down on the yellow and green fields.

The patchy, grassy fields were stained and bright with birds,
Corn, mossy walking paths and bugs scurrying to find food and a house.
Willow trees dance and sway in the wind.

Bright and blooming stars twinkle in the gorgeous night sky.

Emily Kelsall (11)
Winsford High Street CP School, Winsford

The Hot Air Balloon

Flying above all the nature below,
Beautiful fields scattered with greenery,
Flowers covering the gorgeous meadows,
Joyful people who are smiling with glee.

Scenic waterfalls with pretty water,
Lovely rivers with wavy surfaces,
Little sailboats with little wooden oars,
Wonderful blue lakes with great purpose.

Astonishing forests with charming trees,
Tall long woods with adventurous people,
Nature so spectacular with the bees,
Up above you could see fierce eagles.

Muddy floors with almost everything dead,
Flowers dying out as they were not fed.

Ethan F (11)
Winsford High Street CP School, Winsford

The Hot Air Balloon

Dancing among the hazy morning clouds,
The floating goliath peered on the land.
Hovering above the tall swaying trees,
Branches like fingers leant o'er the river.

Celestial face shines over the river,
Sun-kissed with sliding streams of bright light.
As the clear river splashed against the glistening rocks
It sparkles like white stars in the sunlight.

Rivers are brilliant blue snakes,
Winding through life.
The rivers flow gracefully,
To their ocean home.

Giants cast their eyes over lands below.
Suns of the world are like heaven's sun.

Jainabou K (11)
Winsford High Street CP School, Winsford

Balloon In The Sky

Twirling with clouds in the morn sky,
A ballerina above a sage lawn,
Flying in tunes, a dancer next to clear a lake,
Swaying in rose skies, geese on rocky, grey hills.

A delicate blue butterfly flew high,
Like a dot in the sky,
Flowers so many, so frail, so fair,
Orchids, daffodils, freesia, harebells.

Balloons, so many, so colourful and pretty,
Pink, blue, green, yellow, a patchwork quilt,
A moth so frail but strong and small,
Tall as a skyscraper but colourful as a rainbow.

Kissing the fields with colour,
Balloons so big and delightful.

Paige Walker (11)
Winsford High Street CP School, Winsford

A Journey Through The Sun

Prancing through the atmosphere,
It seemed as if vivid songbirds migrated,
Towards the sovereign eye and over,
Mountain peaks with grace and unity.

Oscillating with comfort along clouds,
They hovered over dells and boughs,
Travelling with ease o'er the sun's rays,
Migrating geese took o'er the airspace.

The rockets rose rapidly onto the hills,
Pride along their spherical tops,
In the spangled, murky skies ready,
For nightfall to erupt on them to seek.

Nighttime has woken from its slumber,
When will you rise again, old friend?

Lillian Majewski (11)
Winsford High Street CP School, Winsford

The Hot Air Balloon

When the large, vibrant birds are set free,
The people below begin to fade away,
All you can see is some large green trees,
And a celestial, golden face.

A collage of flowers dancing proudly,
In all shades of pink, yellow and blue,
Towering trees reaching up high,
Stood firmly against the warm breeze.

The beautiful sunset over the horizon,
Painting the sky red and yellow,
Tweeting feathers above everyone else,
Flapping their wings in the zephyr.

But when it turns night the wind starts to howl,
And the rain smashes against the windows.

Alana Griffin (11)
Winsford High Street CP School, Winsford

The Colourful Titans

At the crack of dawn,
A goliath of many colours arose from his eternal
slumber.
As he took flight,
A dance amongst the clouds on the blue dance,
called the sky, had begun.

Below him was a crashing waterfall,
Cascading to a sudden collision.
A swarm of inflated behemoths had taken to the
air,
Forming a miniature galaxy,
Full of wandering planets trying to reach their star.

Just before his return to rest,
He crossed over a thousand trees blooming with
life,
A million ants scurried on the land, returning to
their nest,
One hot air on the ground.

Caleb Crawford (11)
Winsford High Street CP School, Winsford

As She Drifts Away

With gentle movements,
The balloon rises with colossal height,
She floats on her merry way,
As she leaves the crowds in dismay.

A thin river in the form of a twirling ribbon,
Navigating herself enthusiastically,
As she stays afloat she peers out to the bird's eye
view,
She looks down at the universe's beautiful life.

The illuminated ombre sky scatters cotton candy
clouds,
As sunset slowly descends, clovers and millennial
pink dahlias gain a golden hue.

Alas, the day must come to an end
As she descends to the ground mesmerised.

Lena Sniezek (11)
Winsford High Street CP School, Winsford

The Balloon's Journey Through Nature's Paradise

Colossal balloon full of care,
Awoke into the hazy morning dew.
Pirouetting in the breezy air,
Patchwork goliath surveys the view.

Hundreds of feet in the air, it encounters,
Green grass that is full of buttercups,
Luscious waterfalls cascade down mountains,
Sun's celestial face winks as it rises up.

Titan-like trees create a blanket,
Of shadow knitted by Mother Nature.
Berry pink blossoms bloom from winding vines,
Fairy anemones dance carelessly.

Upon the small flickers of sunrise rays,
Beautiful violets linger around.

Imogen Gabbott (11)
Winsford High Street CP School, Winsford

Flying And Floating

Thy blood red orb dances in the skies of blue,
Below lay hills of emerald green,
Waterfalls dripping with dreams,
Verdant green grass covered with flowers,
Saxe streams that run with passion.

The eye of the sky falls like a ball,
The sun is saying bye and the moon says hi,
Thy moon is here while the sun is in its slumber.

The orb is dancing with the wind in sync,
Now the wind pushes it away with regret,
The orb's fiery heart blows away,
The orb is stuck in trees of green.

O' wind, why did you abandon this poor balloon?

Amelia Bebbington (11)
Winsford High Street CP School, Winsford

Journey Of The Hot Air Balloon

Nervously, the hot air balloon sets off,
Over the luxurious waterfalls.

Water splashing into a colossal trough,
Hot air balloons in the sky moving,
Moving up, down, left and right all night,
In the blue sky they groan,
Throughout the day and night.

The patchwork bees leaving their hive,
Over the hills and through the mountains,
You will find a hot air balloon,
Gliding into the never-ending blue,
Into the cotton candy clouds.

Then it starts to go down as it goes cold,
It lands, that's the story of the hot air balloon.

James Sheppard (11)
Winsford High Street CP School, Winsford

The Hot Air Balloon

The hot air balloon blowing through the sky
Seeing the little cars racing around
Also seeing the little people watching take-off
Going higher, higher and higher
Waving goodbye to the world and going up

Soon taking off to space
Past the clouds
Silently flying through the sky

Miles and miles of open fields
Turn eventually into dark secret forests
Above the trees a sprinkle of icing sugar
Rising to the towering peaks
A blast of hot roaring fire
The journey is nearly over
Tiny ants coming closer
I'm almost near.

Rileigh Bennion (11)
Winsford High Street CP School, Winsford

The Colourful Balloon

Dancing with the milky, fluffy clouds,
The flaming, hot, sparkly sun was setting in the
distance,
Flocks of birds singing past the colourful ball,
The football was kicked in the air.

Kissing with the golden face in the air,
A gushing quick waterfall,
Glancing through the graceful wind,
Hard, mossy field below the ball.

The colossal cliffs shine with the sun,
A fairy flying in the dancing wind,
Hung over the mossy cliffs,
Marvellous rose skies.

The sparkling stars shining on the ball,
The balloon was slowly melting.

Imogen Spencer (11)
Winsford High Street CP School, Winsford

The Hot Air Balloon Journey

With caution, a colossal patchwork balloon rose like warm dough in the oven. Hot air balloon, a jubilant eagle flying over the luscious waterfalls below.
Goliath balloon looming over.
The towering trees beneath it.
A blimp flying over his nest,
Soaring majestically above the rest.
Tiny planets cruising through the never-ending blue.
Beacons of hope floating through the air.
Moth orchids linger embracing minimal sunlight.
Wandering animals are ants scuttling.
Moving left, right, all night.
A floating sphere surveying the picturesque landscape below.

Reece Tucker (11)
Winsford High Street CP School, Winsford

The Hot Air Balloon

Soaring titans are scanning beautiful, majestic
landscapes below,
A golden face forms a magical beam of light o'er
lively grass below,

Waving trees hover above mythical meadows,
Flourishing blossoms mildly blue,
Inching o'er a crystal clear lagoon,
Flowers sit beside flowing streams,

Forlorn clouds separating from each other in a
gorgeous, glimmering, gilded sunset,
The giant observed the cows and sheep on the
green, glorious fields below,

Sunrise brings a new day and a new life,
Colourful birds chirp and striped foxes run.

Alfie P (11)
Winsford High Street CP School, Winsford

The Hot Air Balloon

Celestial golden face shimmers bright,
On green, luscious meadows, there comes daisies,
Flowing diamond rivers gleam in the light,
Like diamonds below, shining on fairies,

Fragile flowers dancing in the gentle breeze,
Soft, sparkling clouds collide in the blue sky,
Forcing all the animals to freeze,
Beautiful rose petals fly by,

Heavenly white clouds,
Match the angels at starlight,
Fog pushes through crowds,
Ocean waves are beautiful, bizarre sights,

Showering rain and grey skies,
Looks deep into sad eyes.

Daisy Skillicorn (11)
Winsford High Street CP School, Winsford

The Hot Air Balloon

With caution, the colossal patchwork balloon,
Rose like a titan awakening from its slumber,
Pink blossom decorated the trees,
Blue waterfalls from the top of the mountains,
Tall sunflowers reached for the sky,
The golden-faced sun shone onto the trees,
Tiny planets floated across the sky.

I watched how the daffodils danced in the wind,
Green grass covered the land like the ocean,
Hot air balloon, are bees leaving the hive?
Colourful space waved as they set off.
Blue sky went darker,
Beautiful stars appeared in the sky.

Amelia Potts (11)
Winsford High Street CP School, Winsford

The Hot Air Balloon

Crystal water dripping down the mountains
Whilst the golden, sacred treasure lurks behind like
a golden face o'er the river
The puffy clouds drift slowly like a snail.

Flowers on the meadows look up at me like
dragons' eyes
While air whistles in my ear
The little towns standing and looking up at the
titans.

The leaves rustling in the breeze
Falling off branches.
While the apples from apple trees fall and roll
Down the green, steep hill.

The charcoal night where no colours, no humans
outside and no sun.

Sebastian G (11)
Winsford High Street CP School, Winsford

The Hot Air Balloon

The floating skyscraper danced in the breeze,
As a golden-faced kissed gilded stream's,
Heavenly light casts beams over patchwork fields,
Glaring over the swaying trees below.

In the hazy morning white blossoms,
Spread all over marvellous meadows
That turns green to gold,
By a fiery sunset.

Floating among the misty morning clouds,
Over arches of fields.
Green and yellow stitched together
As fields spangled with flowers.

The trees that spangled the leaves sway,
Here comes winter for today.

Riley T (11)
Winsford High Street CP School, Winsford

The Big Hot Air Balloon

A family of four stepped on the balloon,
With bravery and fear,
They uplifted from the venust grass,
The family were hoisted in the air.

They had made it to the balloon's highest point,
As they were unmoving,
They took all of the view in their heart,
As the group laughed and smiled they ate their picnic.

When they had finished eating they started declining.
As the family were landing,
They were all laughing,
They hit the ground.

All of them got off,
They had fun in the car and went home.

Laiton Haspell (11)
Winsford High Street CP School, Winsford

The Hot Air Balloon

Dancing among the hazy morning clouds,
The glistening goliath shone above the mountains,
The fields gaze up in colossal amazement.
The glistening clear water.

Plunged into a black hole.
It danced around the spangled towering titans,
Which showered among
The shimmering colour collage in the air.

The ball planed across the air furiously.
The fire was shouting monstrously.
The mysterious, calming goliath,
Gazed across the patchwork grassy fields.

The floating pop of colour,
Surveyed the land.

Lola Lowndes (11)
Winsford High Street CP School, Winsford

The Hot Air Balloon

A giant patchwork balloon,
Rising up like a kite,
Floating through fluffy cotton candy clouds,
Looking down on the pink blossoming trees,
Surveying the landscape below.

Like tiny planets soaring through endless blue,
Casting shadows over clear blue rivers twisting
through caves and mountains,
Wandering animals appear like ants scuttling from
one place to another.

Little beacons of hope,
On a journey through the air,
Flying over golden daffodils and red roses,
Moth orchids linger embracing minimal sunlight.

Nicole Jones (11)
Winsford High Street CP School, Winsford

The Hot Air Balloon

What a glorious morning I have seen.
Shining on the meadows is where it lay.
The sun is beautiful, dancing as they sway.
With daisies and roses that stay.

Lovely blossoms pounce and sway where I lie.
In the shade is where I hate most.
It's sad because they don't shine in December.

Floating through a heavenly landscape
The peaceful rivers danced in the misty wind
Through the gliding streams
Fish swim all day.

While summer fades winter comes
Pools out and beach trips all gone.

Mia-Grace Bannaghan (10)
Winsford High Street CP School, Winsford

The Hot Air Balloon

Floating colourful giants dance,
Across rose gold sunsets.
They hover above snake-like rivers,
Crashing against heavenly rocks.

A golden face shines upon green meadows,
Decorated with beautiful blossoms,
Flowing fields with rushing rivers,
Move back to their ocean home.

Trees are watching over sacred nature,
Blossoms spreading over the meadows,
The blossoms look like candyfloss,
Scattered across the ground.

The peaceful sunset settled,
As the night got darker.

Laila Hornsby (11)
Winsford High Street CP School, Winsford

The Hot Air Balloon

A colossal patchwork balloon,
Rose like a titan awakening from its slumber,
A shadow was cast over,
The meandering rivers.

Sun-pierced silences filled the sky,
As the balloon navigated around,
Moth orchids linger embracing minimal sunlight,
Luscious waterfalls splashed,
Their way through the hilltops.

When the balloon appeared at night,
It dazzled in the skylight,
Tiny plants hovered around while
The pink blossom decorated the trees
As Goliath surveyed the landscape.

Maisy Newton (11)
Winsford High Street CP School, Winsford

The Hot Air Balloon

Dancing from head to toe,
Among the hazy morning clouds,
The floating hot air balloon,
Was high into the sky.

It cast its gaze across the fields,
Of green and yellow stitched together
By the thread of the hedgerows.
The clouds looked very puffed out.

The bright sun was gazing with sunlight,
The grass was bright green,
The sky was light blue
And the trees were as clear as a breeze.

The weather was stunning with sunlight,
Just the way everyone liked it.

Lola Talbot (11)
Winsford High Street CP School, Winsford

The Hot Air Balloon

Balloons danced through clusters of frail coral
clouds,
A large expanse of forests coated the large
balloons' vision.

Intricate patchwork spheres rose further up into
the gleaming sky,
They flew through the sky in a manner that
resembled a bird leading its flock.

Coloured fabric drifted past a fluorescent ball of
light,
When the balloon gazed down on people looking
up it only rose higher.

The hot air balloon floated down from the
kaleidoscopic sunrise and down to the hazy fields.

Erin L (11)
Winsford High Street CP School, Winsford

The Land Below

Luscious waterfalls cascade off the grassy hilltop below,
Woodpeckers peek,
Peck at the luxurious willow trees.

Hot air balloons dancing through the cotton candy clouds,
Colossal rivers weave around the soaring trees,
Hot air balloons like bees leaving their hive.

Glistening water reflects the teal sky above pink blossoms,
Blossoms decorate the ground below,
Patchworked balloons like titans roaming the sky.

Wandering animals roaming,
Roaming the ground below us.

Jaicob Wilcock (11)
Winsford High Street CP School, Winsford

The Hot Air Balloon

A colossal, patchwork balloon,
Rose like giants awakening,
Like bees leaving their hives,
Tiny planets gliding across the daylight sky,
From above being admired down below it awaits.

Blue river drifting below,
Casting shadows linger above,
When balloons appear at night,
Embracing the moonlight,
With stars hovering around.

Tiny planets dance around,
While the night flies around so fast,
Daylight comes,
Pink blossom painting the trees so beautifully.

Bella Doyle (11)
Winsford High Street CP School, Winsford

The Hot Air Balloon

Dancing among the hazy morning clouds
The floating goliath surveyed the land
Patchwork fields are green and yellow
Stitched together by the thread of hedgerows

The hot air balloon is a glowing giant
Protecting its land, the hot air balloon is
Alone floating in the sky

It watched animals scavenging for food
The hot air balloon waved at everyone
And they waved back
Diving towards the point of start

Happy, it lifts hearts
It lights souls.

Oliver W (11)
Winsford High Street CP School, Winsford

The Hot Air Balloon

Upon the lovely clouds,
Lies an anxious balloon,
It listens to nature's sounds,
While nearing closer to the ground,
Or it looks for the world unfound.

When the stars come out,
Most children cry and pout,
The balloon glimmers in the night,
While it hides behind the moon that shines so
bright.

It glides over the meadows nurs'd in dew,
This balloon must fulfil his quest,
To travel north, east, south and west,
Now he can finally rest.

Max Beech (11)
Winsford High Street CP School, Winsford

The Hot Air Balloon

It is a majestic creature,
That flies across the sky.
It blends in with the dancing colours,
Of light and night.

It soars across the green waves,
That glisten in the day.
It listens to the birds in the night,
And the ones that shine in moonlight.

The sound of critters,
Having fun in the sun.
Twirl in my ears it's all good fun,
They laugh and they tweet and twirl and they spin.

As it floats to the start,
It melts my heart.

Caitlin Johnston (10)
Winsford High Street CP School, Winsford

The Hot Air Balloon

A colossal patchwork balloon,
Rising like dough in the oven.
Dancing between the misty clouds,
The floating goliath surveyed the rich scenery
beneath.
It cast its gaze across patchwork meadows of
emerald green and yellow.

Tiny planets floated across the sky,
Its shadow was cast over meandering rivers which
flowed beneath.
Animals popped up, ants scuttled from their nest
And pink blossom decorated the landscape.
Waterfalls stood out in the blazing sky.

Lolah Batin (11)
Winsford High Street CP School, Winsford

The Hot Air Balloon

Dancing among the hazy clouds as dawn rose
The gigantic titans galloped through the air
As the bright yellow sun stained the earth
Among the hazy morning clouds
The floating goliath surveyed the land.

It casts its gaze across the patchwork fields
Green, yellow, stitched together by hedgerow
thread
A hot air balloon
Is a lone petal in the sky.

The hot air balloon is a glowing giant
Protecting its land as
They tower over humanity.

Isaac B-S (11)
Winsford High Street CP School, Winsford

The Hot Air Balloon

Dancing among the fluffy clouds,
The big goliath surveying the land of high.
The colourful balloon,
With lovely yellow and green.

The colossal, colourful canvas,
Glided over the lake,
The water swelling
Through the cold breeze.

The cloudy, foggy mountains,
Standing still like a statue in the breeze.
The spring hedgehogs searching,
For food and a home.

The moon is going down,
And the sun is rising for a new day.

Paige Marsh (11)
Winsford High Street CP School, Winsford

The Hot Air Balloon

Dancing among the hazy clouds,
The giant balloon watched over
Creating a shadow blanket
Across the glossy fields.

The hot air balloon is a lone petal,
Floating in the bright sky.
The gliding goliath,
Shaped as a pear,

Looked over animals,
Scavenging for food
It cast its gaze across patchwork meadows
Green, yellow, stitched together by hedgerow
thread.

The hot air balloon waved,
At anyone who went past.

Isobel Stott (11)
Winsford High Street CP School, Winsford

The Hot Air Balloon

Dancing among the hazy clouds
We surveyed the land
It cast its gaze
We saw small mini cars

The hot air balloon
Carefully it bloomed
With the air and breeze
And it blew in the bright sky
Filled the sky with clouds
And below it was green, wet patchwork

As it went down we started getting closer to the
ground
It felt odd
Together we landed safe and sound
It felt weird to be on the floor
No more air.

Mya Winnington (10)
Winsford High Street CP School, Winsford

The Eye Of The Airship

Fluttering among the towering, glossy mountains,
With humanity looking below.
The balloon is the rose petal of the sky,
So pink and fresh.

It gazes upon some tiny cars,
Racing below.
Water tumbles down hills,
Like a speed boat.

The airship lingered,
Upon the shiny, sunny sky.
Looking up at the jocund birds,
Fluttering through the air.

Drifting homeward now,
Looking for the green patchwork fields.

Amelia Moore (11)
Winsford High Street CP School, Winsford

The Hot Air Balloon

Dancing from the hazy morning clouds,
Hot air balloons flying above the awaiting cities,
The floating goliath surveyed the land from afar,

Fairies in the sky,
It cast its gaze across the patchwork fields of
green and yellow
Stitched together by the thread of the hedgerows,

The weather is like heaven before your eyes,
Fireworks waking into the early, dull sky,

The clouds were puffy, white and soft,
It was marvellous.

Grace Pattinson (11)
Winsford High Street CP School, Winsford

Big Hot Balloon

Dancing among the hazy morning clouds,
The bright blue balloon glides through the cool,
fresh air,
Surveying the emerald green, grassy fields,
Almost touching the huge, mossy mountain.

The floating goliath flew with tiny kites among the
clouds,
With its fellow big, round balloons,
It soared over the white, misty clouds,
The round balloon sailed into the orange sunset,
The spangled star flew with the clouds in the night
sky.

Jaiden Y (11)
Winsford High Street CP School, Winsford

The Hot Air Balloon

The floating frail balls stroll in the humid air
High in the sky it is a flair.

Overshadowing the cars, fields and trees
500 feet below
Gliding in the air with a flow.

Diving past mountains and fountains
And making famous peaks look like hills
Lingering through cities and towns
Towering the buildings and people who were
shocked.

Gazing in the moon
It was bound to be sunrise soon.

Reuben Coleman (11)
Winsford High Street CP School, Winsford

The Hot Air Balloon

Flying across the fair
The colossal titan watched over the land
The colours blinded the people below
The patchwork stitched up brilliantly

Dancing among the hazy clouds
Fields green and yellow
Stitched together
It cast its gaze
It surveyed the land
It danced
It rose higher
Come towards a marvellous mountain

Then stopping
In water.

Isaac B (11)
Winsford High Street CP School, Winsford

Hot Air Balloon

Dancing among the moon sky
The flying canvas lands from the high sky
Gaze across the air
River through the narrows and through the clouds
High sky to high by

Great balloons hound at fast pace
Gazing through the sky with balloons

Great mood means great wounds
Fast pace, more space, more grace
For the sky to go bye.

Joseph R (11)
Winsford High Street CP School, Winsford

Nature

Nature is something that should be saved,
It's not a place where plastic is made,
Trees give oxygen and CO2,
It's what I breathe in and out and so do you.

Trees will be made into chairs and tables,
Maybe houses and sometimes stables,
The trees are cut down, across the nations
It's a well-known thing called deforestation.

The Amazon is the biggest forest,
There might be no future, let's be honest,
And no future is a massive thing,
We've got to act before the trees start
disappearing.

James Doster (10)
Ysgol Gynradd Gymunedol Gymraeg Llantrisant, Miskin

Flying Away

Walking home with my duck family,
See the sky right in front of me,
I want to go up with my family,
But sadly I'm down here very lonely.

Going up is the goal,
But I flew into a pole and landed in a hole
Then I saw something in the hole...
A ham roll!

I ate the ham roll,
And got out of the hole,
1, 2, 3 and up,
I was in the air with my family!

Belle Htut (11)
Ysgol Gynradd Gymunedol Gymraeg Llantrisant, Miskin

YOUNG WRITERS INFORMATION

We hope you have enjoyed reading this book – and that you will continue to in the coming years.

If you're the parent or family member of an enthusiastic poet or story writer, do visit our website **www.youngwriters.co.uk/subscribe** and sign up to receive news, competitions, writing challenges and tips, activities and much, much more! There's lots to keep budding writers motivated!

If you would like to order further copies of this book, or any of our other titles, then please give us a call or order via your online account.

Young Writers
Remus House
Coltsfoot Drive
Peterborough
PE2 9BF
(01733) 890066
info@youngwriters.co.uk

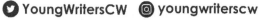 

 YoungWritersUK
 YoungWritersCW youngwriterscw

Scan me to watch the Poetry Towers video!